What Du
about

<u>Novels by Elizabeth Musser</u>

The Secrets of the Cross Trilogy:

Two Crosses

Two Testaments

Two Destinies

The Swan House

The Dwelling Place

Searching for Eternity

Words Unspoken

The Sweetest Thing

Waiting for Peter

****

ELIZABETH MUSSER

MacGregor *Literary*

Waiting for Peter
Originally Published in Dutch
for The Week of the Christian Book, 2009
by Uitgeverij Voorhoeve

Copyright © 2008
Elizabeth Musser

First English Printing 2014

Cover Photo of Beau by Sylvain Felix

ISBN 978-1-932496-97-0

Dedication

In memory of our neurotic mutt, Beau, who was adopted on September 11, 1999 and enriched our lives until his last breath, December 31, 2012. I thank my Lord for putting him in our lives and for all that I learned about my Master from Beau.

About the Author

ELIZABETH GOLDSMITH MUSSER, an Atlanta native and the bestselling author of The Swan House, is a novelist who writes what she calls 'entertainment with a soul.' For over twenty five years, Elizabeth and her husband, Paul, have been involved in missions work with International Teams. They presently live near Lyon, France. The Mussers have two sons, a daughter-in-law and a grandson.

To learn more about Elizabeth and her books, and to find discussion questions as well as photos of sites mentioned in the stories, please visit www.elizabethmusser.com.

Prologue

The day is almost boiling hot, so that my tongue hangs out of my mouth and I pant, my sides heaving in and out, in and out. I lay on the hot pavement of the driveway, my ears pricked forward, my eyes attentive, my heart racing—not only from the heat, but from hope. Perhaps this will be the day he returns. Perhaps, in just a short moment, I will catch his scent on the faintest breeze and hear his uneven step as he walks up the driveway.

I have waited for so long. Sometimes, when I hear those distant sounds, I hurry to my feet, although 'hurry' is a different word to me now than when I first came to live with them all those years ago. I stand, prick my ears and lift my muzzle to the wind. They think I am dignified when I do this, and beautiful. They always are calling me beautiful. Or bad dog. One or the other.

I am waiting, but he does not come. My ears sag and I remember all the joyful reunions with him in the past—how we jumped and played and ran. Now it is almost impossible for me to jump in the air or rush to the fence. Even barking takes effort.

I wonder if he will come before it is too late. I am not sure what 'too late' means, only that Bucky is no longer playing next door. I watched the neighbors bury him in their yard, right under the hydrangea bushes.

I only want one thing: to see My Boy again before I too take my spot in the ground.

And so I wait.

Chapter 1

He came to me in early autumn. I was lying in the Cage, ill with distemper, while a dozen other male strays bounced around, yapping madly at the young boy who approached us. Yap, yap, yap! I was tired and sick. One look at me, a good look, showed all my ribs, even through my long hair.

He came right up to the wire fence and knelt down to where I lay.

He whispered something to me and I liked the sound of his voice, the way it cracked a little. I liked not just his voice, full of compassion, but I liked his eyes, round and inquisitive, the color of the end of a summer day, liquid with expression, with life. He was not like many of the children who came to stare at the Cage—loud and whiney and hyperactive. He was calm—too calm for his youth, perhaps, but I did not know about his past then. All I knew was that I liked him, and I wanted him to choose me.

We lived in hierarchy in the Cage, and I was not the lead dog. I lay low and tried to avoid the snarls and bared teeth. We all wanted to get out of the Cage, to find freedom, although we knew not where or what.

He had curly blond hair, almost covering his ears, and dark eyes and he laughed, low and smooth, when I licked at his hand which he had placed on the wire fence that separated us. I tasted salt, I tasted warmth and that particular consistency of humanness—kindness and care—that I had once tasted on the hands of the Little Boy and the Weak Woman before the Bad Man stole it all away. I knew this boy would never turn into a Bad Man.

I can read eyes, especially when a human squats down on his haunches and looks directly at me. That's how I know who will be bad and who will be good and who will simply not care. In my life before I came to the Cage, I had known one of each of these types of humans.

The boy laughed softly and looked down at me and I raised my head and looked at him. Our eyes connected, and I began to wag my tail, slowly, only a flop, flop against the bare pavement, but he saw it.

He turned around to speak with a woman, while pointing at me. Later, I would come to love her eyes too. Later, I would want to protect her, but on this particular day with my future being decided by a nod or shake of her head, all I wanted was for the boy to convince the woman to take me with them.

One part of the woman's mouth turned up slightly, her eyes became liquid and she nodded. I knew then that I had found the meaning of a word they used so often at this place. A Home.

Chapter 2

One year and six days after the accident, I took Peter to the Humane Society. We had already visited the pet store, but Peter was adamant. "I don't want to buy a puppy, Mom. I want to adopt one. I want to get a dog who needs me."

What Peter didn't say, but what I heard nonetheless, was that he wanted a dog who had suffered as he had, who could understand him. Peter was always like that, a sensitive soul.

So on a muggy afternoon in early September I drove him to the Humane Society, just the two of us—our outing—and the rest of the family understood, did not ask to come along. This was going to be Peter's dog, and maybe, just maybe, this dog was going to change Peter's life. Bring him back to us. We were all holding our breaths, figuratively, of course, and praying—very literal and fervent prayers—that a dog might be able to reach that wounded spot inside of Peter that no human had been able to touch—not me, not his father or his sisters, not the counselor, not dear Dr. Reuben who had known our family at that time for over fifteen years and had, in fact, brought Peter into the world.

On that Wednesday afternoon, I already had a headache and the incessant barking of dogs immediately compounded it as we walked through the heavy metal doors and were greeted by long wire cages filled with frantic dogs. Hundreds of them, it seemed to me, of every size and shape, many of them motley looking.

I had promised Peter that he could choose, alone. So I stood off to the side and watched my twelve-year-old son wind in and out of the rows and rows of cages. He walked slowly, so that the limp was barely noticeable, with determination, taking everything in, as he always did. The dogs greeted him boisterously, excitedly, desperately.

Peter was methodical. I knew not to rush him. So I found a seat on a stone bench near the office and I waited. I think that so much of a mother's life is waiting. Waiting to become pregnant, waiting for the baby inside to make his appearance, waiting to find out that he is perfect and healthy, waiting for him to do all the things he is supposed to do at the right time during his early years, waiting for him to learn and mature. Waiting for him to come home.... But I digress.

After an hour-long search through cages, Peter made his choice: the long-haired red dog with the eyes that matched his coat and fur so soft it seemed to belong on a Persian cat. He was in the very last cage in the kennel. So often, waiting pays off.

I think Peter knew he was the one as soon as he saw him. The dog, a male, was lying down while a dozen other dogs danced around him. They leapt onto the wire fence; they barked and ran and snapped and wagged their tails, they shrieked—if dogs can shriek—begging Peter to look at them. A few showed their fangs and Peter immediately moved to the end of the cage, where the red dog lay, looking, quite frankly, pitiful.

The red dog did not stand. He just whined at Peter and his bushy tail wagged barely, flopping on the urine-soaked cement. He had the sweetest and softest rust-colored eyes, as sweet and as soft as Peter's. There they sat, Peter squatting down, oblivious to the other dogs, his hand pushed against the wire fencing, and the dog reaching his neck forward, his tongue coming out and licking Peter's hand through the wire.

I think that was the moment they became inseparable.

"I want this one, Mom," he whispered, cleared his voice and said again, "This one."

I did not answer at once because my first reaction would have been to point out that this dog looked sick, very sick. I did not want Peter to become attached to an animal who might die in the weeks to come. I wanted to protect my son from any more disappointments, at least for the immediate future.

But I believed in prayer and I believed in my son, so I bit my tongue, gave him a half grin—which always meant 'yes'—and simply said, "Okay."

We went inside to the office and talked to the volunteer worker. When we pointed out the one Peter had chosen, she said, "He's a sweet dog; he has a good temper. He hasn't been here too long—a month or two. Someone found him in a parking lot—must have run away.

He'd been beaten. Looked like it was with a big piece of wood. Poor, scared thing."

"He was hurt?" Peter asked. Peter never talked to strangers.

"Yes."

That was that. The dog's fate was sealed. He was ours.

The other dogs yapped wildly as he left his cage. Somehow they knew that he had been chosen. I wondered if dogs felt jealousy.

We bought a collar and a leash right there and Peter put them around the dog's neck and led him out of the cage. As he stood, I saw that the dog, though scrawny, was not small. He was, in fact, over medium height, the size of a setter. I remembered vaguely our family discussion that we wanted a small, short-haired dog.

Immediately the meek and mild dog—barely a year old, they estimated—began to yank and bark and jump and pull. Weak and sick, perhaps, but the dog was determined when he put his mind to it.

Peter got him in the back seat by picking him up awkwardly. I almost said, "Watch out, honey. You never know—he might bite." But I refrained. The dog did not bite Peter. Instead, he trembled and shook, as Peter took a seat beside him and repeated over and over, "It's okay, fella." I glanced back often as I chauffeured the two of them home. Twice the dog peed on the back seat of the car, but I didn't say a word because, before we got home, the dog lay on the seat, his head in Peter's lap, and my son looked like he had at last found a true friend. Peter had gotten what he dreamed of: a dog who needed him.

Chapter 3

The first human I ever met was a woman—I can tell the difference by the smell and the voice. She was the one who fed my mother and watched the puppies, six of us, as we nursed voraciously. I remember smelling the human scent and wondering what it was. I was not afraid of it, simply curious. Puppies are curious. I had not yet learned to be afraid, not yet met the Bad Man.

Mother licked us—always licking—a lick of love. My mother was a beautiful dog, what humans call a Brittany spaniel. She had a fine, long muzzle and intelligent eyes and her coloring, white with rusty splotches all over her body, was the mark of a purebred. She wasn't a large dog, measuring about a foot and a half by human standards. She was in every way a pedigreed dog, but I did not know this at the time.

I also did not know that this particular litter of puppies was a big disappointment to the Humans. We were a 'mistake', mutts. Evidently, my mother escaped, as she was prone to do while she was in heat, and so, instead of being bred to one of the top Brittany spaniels in the region, she ended up mating with the playboy of the neighborhood, a big bastard who was a haphazard cross between an Irish setter, a golden retriever and a few other breeds, far removed.

The result of this liaison was us, six scrawny puppies, two short-haired and spotted like my mother, two short-haired and tan, like neither parent, one pure white with a spaniel look and me, the red one, the one who looked most like my father. Though a mutt and a playboy, my father had a reputation among humans as being 'one of the most beautiful dogs' they had ever seen.

My life for a while was food and brothers and sisters and more food and tumbling and high-pitched yelps and stern looks from the human man and the human woman who fed us and who were, so we gathered, severely disappointed in us. I did not understand this at the time, but years later, I learned from other dogs and from life, that we were not worth much money—a very important thing for humans—and that the Bad Man and the Weak Woman only wished to get rid of us as quickly as possible.

Two of my brothers were taken away quite early. A family of humans came and looked at all of us and the little girl and little boy petted us and laughed and finally they picked out my brothers, the tan ones. My mother and my other brother and sisters and I had no idea what was happening. A small human hand, belonging to the boy, picked them up and put them in a very strange contraption for moving places—humans rarely use their legs if they can help it. Then off they went. We never saw my brothers again.

A few other people came to look at us, but they never took any of us. We wanted to stay with our mother, which suited us just fine, but the Weak Woman seemed worried. The Little Boy—who belonged to the Weak Woman and the Bad Man—liked me best. How a dog looks is something that matters a lot to humans, and I looked 'beautiful' to him. He cuddled me at night before he went to his room, and I was glad and I licked his hand just as Mother licked me.

Sometimes, the Bad Man came into the garage where I stayed with my mother and brother and sisters. The Bad Man was big and heavy and he smelled funny all the time, different from the other humans. He smelled of a particular liquid that was often lying around the house in bottles and cans. He had Mean Eyes and we puppies knew that the Little Boy was scared of the Bad Man.

Dogs can smell fear. I smelled it on the Little Boy and the Weak Woman.

The Little Boy and the Weak Woman left every morning and didn't come home until the sun was very high in the sky. The Bad Man stayed at the house and lay on the sofa surrounded by his bottles and cans.

One day, the Awful Day, he came into the garage where we stayed and he grabbed up my brother and sisters and put them in a big cloth bag—just threw them in. They started howling and yapping and he yelled at them. He headed out the door with my mother chasing him. She did not like the Bad Man, but she also was afraid of him. We all were. Once he had kicked at my mother.

He kept walking away and my mother ran after him, barking frantically, leaping at the Sack where my brother and sisters were slung over his shoulder. Finally he set down the Sack—really threw it down hard—and turned on my mother. She backed up, barking and showing her fangs—something she had never done before. He came toward her with a stick, swinging it back and forth, and hit her hard on the haunches, so that she fell down with a loud yelp. Then he grabbed her by the scruff of the neck and dragged her back into the garage and shut the door. Sometimes in my dreams, I can still hear her desperate, frantic yelps.

I had run over to the Sack and was nipping at it, trying to free my brother and sisters when the Bad Man came back. He started swinging the stick at me and I scrambled under a bunch of wood behind the house. He left me alone then.

But I followed him as he took the Sack down to the River. He opened it and I thought he was going to take out my brother and sisters and let them drink, but he didn't. He started putting big rocks in the Sack, many big rocks. I could hear them yelping. Then he tied the Sack closed and swung it with all his might into the River. I watched the splash and heard their yelps and then nothing.

Nothing.

I knew they were gone. The Bad Man had killed them. Mother had told us to be careful about the River, told us it was a dangerous place. I had not understood why. Now I knew.

Later, when the Little Boy and the Weak Woman came home, they let my mother out of the garage and I lay beside her. The Little Boy and the Weak Woman cried when they couldn't find the puppies. This is how humans show they are sad—liquid comes out of their eyes.

No liquid came out of my eyes or Mother's, but my poor mother wouldn't eat for days, not until the Weak Woman took her in her lap and stroked her and fed her from her hands.

I still nursed, but I always kept alert, my ears pricked and my nose turned up, sniffing for the Bad Man. I had several hiding places I ran to whenever he showed up, but after the Awful Day, I never again felt completely safe, especially not around big male humans.

Chapter 4

The Weak Woman and the Little Boy were kind to me. The child was too young to have responsibility to take care of me—although I certainly tried to take care of him. The woman fed me and Mother and taught me a few important lessons, especially where I could go peepee—never ever in the house. I loved to chew up their things. My teeth often hurt and chewing made them feel better. But I learned that humans do not like puppies to chew. In fact, there were many things the humans didn't like for me to do. Simply because I chewed up a shoe or overturned a vase or snatched a piece of bread from a plate that was left low enough for me to reach, they would suddenly become furious and yell the same thing over and over again.

I got bigger and bigger and spent days nipping at Mother and chasing balls and snapping at flies—they are delicious! The Little Boy did not play with me much. He had other things to play with, things that didn't wiggle or bark or jump or fetch balls, things that he could make do whatever he wanted.

Still I was loyal to them, these humans. I even tried to be loyal to the Bad Man. I stayed by the woman's feet whenever she was home, and I tried to take care of her and the boy, especially when the Bad Man was being loud and mean. The Bad Man did not like me at all; he got angry when I barked at him, but I had to warn the Weak Woman and the Little Boy when I smelled that strident smell, not of food, but of something strong and acidic. Whenever he smelled that way, he was mean.

Then one day, the Worst Day of All, he attacked my mother. He was alone with us, drinking his foul-odored liquid and yelling at Mother for getting in his way as he stumbled around the house. He kicked at Mother, which scared her. She showed her fangs and yapped at him to keep his distance, but instead, he picked up a big broom handle and came toward her, swinging it, evil flashing in his eyes. I rushed in and jumped on him, barking and grabbing his legs. I did not want to hurt him, but simply warn him not to go near my mother. He turned on me with the broom handle. He broke it across my head, and I went down with a howl; he beat me again while I was on the ground. Mother lunged at him and he went after her. I struggled to my feet and jumped on the Bad Man, sinking my teeth into his arm. He screamed with pain and then his eyes got fiercer than I had ever seen them before. Mother kept yelping at me to go away, assuring me that the Bad Man knew better than to hurt her—she was worth a lot of money. He beat me again with the broom handle. I thought he had broken my back. I crawled under the house.

Mother found me there, and she whined as she licked me again and again.

When the Weak Woman and the Little Boy came home, they put me in the car and drove me far away and forced me out of the car in a big parking lot. Then the Weak Woman gave me a pat, liquid running down her face. She slammed the door and left. I never saw the Bad Man or the Weak Woman or the Little Boy again. Nor did I ever see Mother again.

I thought I would die on the Worst Day of All. I lay down beside a building and tried to lick my wounds. I missed Mother. I yelped for her, but she did not come. I fell asleep.

The next day, I spent a lot of time smelling for food and searching for water, also dodging cars and avoiding humans. I was terrified to go far. Surely the Little Boy and the Weak Woman would change their minds and come find me. I waited and watched, but they did not come. A car honked at me and the human yelled. I limped away and found a spot beside several trashcans which smelled of food. I managed to knock over one can and wiggle my way into the smells— rotting food and soggy cardboard and a few hard pieces of bread, and empty containers that still had the smell and taste of meat.

While I was licking at the containers, a Kind Woman came to me, coaxed me into her car with some food and brought me to the Cage.

Chapter 5

I did not like the Cage. I felt trapped. At least at the Bad Man's house I could run free in the woods with Mother and smell the rabbits and the squirrels and the scent of dirt and new rain and fresh grass. In the Cage there were only the smells of the other dogs—male dogs, all of them, and most of them mean—and occasionally the whiff of a female dog or a human. The Cage meant getting used to the constant barking of the other male dogs. It meant being careful, paying attention and eating fast. The food was plain and rancid, but I learned to gobble it down in four or five bites, barely taking the time to breathe. Otherwise, some other dog would come over, pick a fight and take my food.

I learned about the hierarchy, and I learned quickly. I was lowest. That meant I had better protect myself. I bared my teeth like Mother had when the Bad Man was in one of his moods, and I growled whenever any of the other dogs approached me. I learned to lie down and ignore the others and sometimes they left me alone.

The Lead Dog was all black and thick. He spent the days barking at us and ordering us around. What could we do, but run back and forth in that long, wire cage, barking and hoping to attract the attention of some human?

Gus was my only friend in the Cage. We watched out for each other. He was a small tan mutt, thick and muscular with the head of a boxer and the body of a bull dog. He actually looked pretty mean. He explained how life worked in the Cage: We stayed there forever and ever unless by some miracle, a human decided to pick us and take us to a place called 'Home.' Gus said that usually a dog was taken Home and disappeared forever. But once in a while, a dog would come back, for different reasons, and we heard the stories of big yards and lots of food and balls to chase and children who hugged them, and we all dreamed, whenever we dared close our eyes, of being chosen to go Home.

When I first arrived, I felt the Cage was a safe place. No human tried to hurt me. In fact, the humans who worked at the Place of Many

Cages seemed to care about the animals, the puppies and dogs, the kittens and cats. They fed us and daily sprayed water on the ground to clean off our excrement. They were kind, but overworked. There were so many of us, every size and shape of dog and cat, all wanting attention, all needing to be chosen, all wanting a Home.

I was not afraid of the humans. I was afraid of the other dogs, the ones who showed their fangs, who nipped and barked. Some were noisy and others were quieter, but we all grew mean and protective of our food and our very lives. I became like the other dogs. I had to. This was survival.

I thought I would never get out of the Cage. It became my world, with its cement floor and tall wire fences. In the Cage, I was always on my guard, always nervous, always trying to protect myself. But I was not very good at it and inevitably, I ended up sick. I got a cough and some of my wounds from the Bad Man took a long time to heal. I grew weaker in the Cage. We all knew that if we stayed at the Cage for too long, especially if we were sick, there was the distinct possibility that we might end up getting the Shot, and that meant no home, no future, The End.

Gus was the one who told me about the Shot. Once he had actually witnessed one of the other dogs receiving the Shot when Gus was in an adjoining room being treated for worms. He said that the Vet held the dog down on a long metal table and took a syringe filled with a liquid and gave the dog the Shot. And right away, the dog stopped moving, only jerked a little and then he was gone. Dead.

But I didn't get the Shot. Instead, My Boy crouched down and looked at me and I got to go Home.

Chapter 6

Peter named the dog Sunset—which was shortened to Sunny—for his color, a deep red-orange, a burning flame; he was pure mutt, but a beautiful one, a cross between a Brittany spaniel, an Irish setter and a golden retriever, as best anyone could tell. He was made to steal hearts and he stole all of ours, that very first day.

When Peter brought him in the house, half-pulling, half-carrying him, the rest of the family was waiting. The dog's ears were flattened against his head and his tail was tucked so far under his back legs that he looked tailless. He slipped on the tile floor in the entrance hall and peed again.

Our daughters came into the hall first. Fran, who was fourteen at the time, immediately fell to her knees beside Peter and hugged the dog around the neck. He took to her quickly, with an uncertain wag of the tail and a lick of the face. Cara, typically aloof at seventeen, broke into a grin and said, "He is absolutely beautiful. Skinny as anything, but gorgeous." She knelt down and petted him. I got my camera out and I still have that picture, Sunny lying on the floor, looking suddenly extremely content, surrounded by Fran and Cara and Peter.

But when my husband, Hudson, came into the hallway, Sunny, trembling, scrambled to his feet and began barking and backing away. The poor dog was terrified.

Hudson is a big man, six feet two and sturdy. He held out his hand to the dog and talked softly, coaxing him. "It's okay, buddy. I'm not going to hurt you. It's okay."

But Sunny barked even more ferociously, his front legs stiff and planted far apart, his head down, sniffing and barking and inching backwards so that he was squashed against Peter's leg, his bushy orange tail again stuck between his legs.

Peter, still on the floor, hugged his dog and petted him and kept saying in his cracking adolescent voice, "It's okay, boy. It's okay. It's just Dad. He won't hurt you."

Hudson knelt down, too, and held out his hand. We would learn with time that this was the only way a big man could approach Sunny: squatting and on eye level. Sunny took one step forward, slipping, tail still thrust between his legs. He stretched his neck as far as he could without moving forward and finally his rust-colored nose touched Hudson's hand. Sunny's ears went back and forth, up and down, and I thought he was using every one of his senses to try to decide, "Can I trust this man?"

Peter looked worried. "Mom, remember the lady at the Humane Society said he'd been mistreated. Maybe that's why he's so afraid."

I nodded. "We'll just need to give him a little time."

Ten minutes later, Sunny was licking Hudson's hand and my husband was shaking his head and saying to me, "Lanie, dear, you two have picked a real keeper. A skinny, sickly, long-haired neurotic dog. That's the last time I let the two of you go to the Humane Society together." But in the end, I sometimes wondered if Hudson didn't love that dog the most of all of us.

Chapter 7

Home was not like the place where the Weak Woman and the Little Boy and the Bad Man lived. I could tell that the humans at Home really wanted me to be there with them, even the Very Big Man, who scared me until he knelt down and let me see his eyes and smell his breath. He was not like the Bad Man. In fact, I soon would find that he was a very Good Man and I grew to love him as much as I loved My Boy and the Good Woman and the Silly Girl and the Temperamental Teen. I came to a Home filled with humans who needed me to love them and protect them.

Excitement does not come near to describing how I felt. From the Bad Man and the Awful Day and the Worst Day of All to the Cage and now to Home. I was rescued and given a boy to love. How I loved him! I owed him everything. He had chosen me! I was content to follow him around all my life, follow My Boy.

How we played together! He loved to throw tennis balls for me to fetch. He tossed them high in the air, and I tried to catch them in my mouth before they hit the ground. Then I took off running with My Boy tearing after me. After a while, we both ended up lying in the sweet smelling grass with the heat of an autumn day on our backs, both panting, both happy simply to be together.

I memorized everything about My Boy: his eyes, his smell, the particular way he walked with an uneven gait—I suppose that he too had been mistreated at some time—and his touch. That was my favorite part, when he came downstairs in the early morn, sullen and bleary-eyed. He'd see me. I'd lift my head and wag my tail and turn over on my back and with one naked foot, My Boy massaged my tummy. And I wondered if any other dog could be as happy and thankful as I was.

Chapter 8

What struck me that first day, after the initial introductions, was that Sunny was immediately loyal to us, immediately ready to trust us with himself, immediately attached, following us from room to room, seemingly content to know we were nearby. He wiggled his body with pleasure to show how thankful he was. He gobbled down his food and lapped up his water with enthusiasm and then he lay down in the shade, content.

He had a reason to be thankful; he'd literally been rescued out of the pit of hell. He was chosen to have a real home and master, to no longer be an abandoned orphan, longing for love, driven by instincts. He was adopted by us. And everything changed. I think he immediately fell in love with our family. His loyalty knew no bounds. In fact, I could get annoyed with the way he followed me around, day in and day out.

But most of the time, I felt simply very thankful to have this red mutt in the house.

He delighted in walks with any member of the family. No wonder—what a relief it must have been to be out of that confining cage. Since we lived in a very small house with a very small fenced-in back yard, taking Sunny on walks was imperative. Actually 'walks' did not adequately describe the experience. They were rather 'runs' or 'pulls'.

On Peter's first walk with Sunny, my son looked confidant and happy, holding Sunny on his leash. No sooner had Peter opened the front door than Sunny yanked the leash and galloped into the front yard and then into the street in front of the house, with Peter yanking back and shouting, "Heel, heel, Sunny!" which accomplished absolutely nothing. I wanted to warn Peter to be careful—that Sunny seemed strong and determined, but I said nothing. And I even found myself giggling as I watched my son, holding up his sagging jeans in one hand and pulling on the leash with the other, disappear around the corner.

Twenty minutes later, Peter returned to the house, flush-faced with a hole in the knee of his jeans and a patch of dried blood on his elbow. He was limping more than usual. "Sunny's not very obedient," he commented. Then my son's somber face broke into a rare grin. "He stopped every two seconds to pee on every single bush around—smelling and then peeing. And then he'd pull me along, and once, as we were crossing the street, another dog on a leash passed us and Sunny lunged at him and jerked the leash out of my hands and he went after that dog. They got into this massive fight, Mom."

"Oh, my!" I had never been very good at not showing surprise.

"It was way cool, Mom. When Sunny jumped on that dog, I lost my balance and fell down. But I got up quick and then I had to pull Sunny off the other dog and I thought I was gonna get bit and then when I finally got them apart, I thought the other dog's owner was gonna kill me. I told her I had just gotten my dog from the animal shelter and that I was awful sorry.

"She didn't even yell at me, Mom. She just picked up her little pooch and said, 'You be careful, young man. I think your dog is very dominant. Maybe you should take him to obedience classes.'" By then, Peter had unsnapped Sunny's leash and the two of them were cuddled on the floor in the kitchen, Peter wolfing down three cookies and giving several to his dog, too. "Isn't that so cool? So can I, Mom?"

"Can you what?"

"Can I take Sunny to obedience school?"

I didn't answer for the longest time. I was witnessing a miracle. My son, who could not do sports and who cried easily when injured, was completely oblivious to his bloody elbow and was smiling. He had actually talked to a stranger and now he actually sounded excited about something. The last time Peter had sounded this excited was about three years earlier, when Hudson had offered to buy him the newest model of Lego if he cut the grass.

I decided then and there that Sunny was indeed a keeper. He was a true gift to us—a very unconventional answer to our prayers sent to us from a benevolent God who had heard this mother's cries of frustration and fear for her son.

Chapter 9

Sunny came to us during a turbulent time in our lives. I was working part time at the public library, finally making use of the Masters in Library Science I had received before Fran was born. Hudson's business had gotten more notice and was actually starting to make more of a profit, which meant he traveled constantly. Thankfully, Cara, at seventeen, had saved up enough money from babysitting and a summer job at McDonald's to help us pay for her to have a car. That was our deal—she paid for half of the car as well as insurance and gas. The car meant that she helped cart Fran to her numerous social obligations and Peter to piano lessons, as well as keeping up with her own busy schedule. These things Cara did begrudgingly. She and I were at a point in our relationship where every word I pronounced she interpreted as accusation. I tried to keep calm, but honestly, I felt like Cara was an accident waiting to happen. In the months before Sunny came to our home, she had become withdrawn and secretive. I think it happened gradually, but I was so preoccupied with Peter and his issues that I didn't notice it until one day I woke up and my enthusiastic, bright and helpful daughter had turned into a witch. No kidding.

For a few months, I tried to wave some kind of magic wand and make her become the sweet daughter of yesteryear, but of course, that didn't work. She was too old to be sent to her room, she ignored my curfews, and often, my nightly talks with Hudson—he would phone me from some hotel in the northeast or Midwest—became all about Cara. I began to resent his traveling, leaving me to deal with the kids.

Fran had a sweet personality, and she usually pitched in to help me with dinner preps and laundry, but that little ray of sunshine was becoming the social queen of the universe and I could not keep up with her. She obeyed the curfews, got her homework done and always greeted me in the morning with a kiss and a "Hi, Mom!" But inside, I had this gnawing fear that I was losing her too, that one day, she would wake up and decide, as Cara had, that I was her enemy.

I have already shared about Peter.

Sunny came to us when the last thing I needed was one more mouth to feed, one more warm body to worry about and keep up with. I certainly did not need a dog that had to be walked in the morning, afternoon and evening. As much as Peter loved his dog, it often fell to me to take Sunny on walks. This became one more thing to add to my already crowded schedule.

Still Sunny brought us much joy in those early weeks. In fact I found my eyes filling with tears whenever I caught Peter splayed out on the floor beside his dog, oblivious to anything around him.

But Sunny caused his share of heartache, too. In fact I sometimes caught myself reviewing all the things he'd done wrong in the short space of five weeks. He had bitten me, so that I had to get a tetanus shot. Granted, he didn't mean to. My leg just happened to get in the way of his mouth as he went after another dog one day on a walk. He tripped me so that I fell so hard on my tailbone that I thought I'd broken it. That left me sitting down with utmost care for a few weeks. He chewed up my brand new garden gloves as well as the watering can, the garden hose, a chair or two, and Peter's baseball cap. He ran away from the park into rush hour traffic with me running desperately after him, sure his next step would be his last. He dashed out of the house when I opened the door to get the mail, savagely attacking a dog on a leash which happened to be walking by at that precise moment. I had to pull the two dogs apart while the other owner, an elderly woman, looked on in shock and horror. Fortunately, neither dog was really hurt.

So during those first days with Sunny I had to make quite a few sacrifices to welcome him into our home (wasn't I already making enough sacrifices for Hudson and the kids?), sacrifices of time, of money, of articles eaten up, of worry and physical pain. But that was the price I gladly paid for the joy that Sunny brought to all of us— Hudson and me and Cara and Fran and Peter. Especially Peter. We all knew from that first day that Sunny would stay with us forever.

Still, I tended to rehearse all the nutty things he'd done in my head, and figuratively pat myself on the back for all my sacrifices. I sometimes even enumerated his crazy antics to friends, which inevitably brought a laugh or two. It was almost as if I held his small sins over his head as a reminder of what a great and kind and loving mistress I was. Fortunately Sunny couldn't understand my twisted reasoning.

It occurred to me one day, as I was bemoaning Cara's latest spar with me and fuming over the way Sunny's bushy tail had accidentally whoosed across the coffee table, causing my favorite vase to crash to the floor and splinter into a thousand pieces, that I was fortunate that my own Master wasn't a bit like me. For more than thirty years I had walked (or stumbled along) with God. If He enumerated all the mistakes I'd made along the way, the list would probably go from here to heaven (or hell). But He didn't keep reminding me of all my small sins. Instead, He asked me to remember His sacrifice and His forgiveness. I contemplated this awesome concept as I was sweeping up the shards of porcelain and quite unexpectedly, I burst into tears. Maybe it was just fatigue and PMS, but I really believe it was conviction.

That mutt was teaching me a lesson! I set down the dust pan and little broom and went to find Sunny. He was cowering under the steps—where he liked to hide after his 'accidents.'

"Sunny, come here," I called to him. He stared at me, those rusty-colored eyes so innocent, his tail flapping tentatively on the floor. He was not about to come out to be punished. Then I got down on the floor in the entrance hall and held out my hand and called again, my voice quivering as I sobbed. I guess he sensed that something was the matter with me. He jumped up and padded over to me, ears attentive, wagging that dangerous tail of his and he plopped down beside me. I rubbed his tummy and said, through my tears, "I forgive you, Sunny."

I'm glad no one was around. The kids would have thought I needed to go to the mental institution. But I think Sunny kind of understood me. He lay there on his back, ears flapped open on the floor, making him look like a bat. His legs were up in the air and he was completely oblivious to the fact that he was displaying his private parts for anyone to see. He had my full attention.

And somehow, sitting there with that mutt, I felt as if I had the Lord's undivided attention too, and He was reminding me again, "I forgive you, Lanie. I love you. Let's just spend a little time together."

Chapter 10

Inevitably, we had to punish Sunny for his misdemeanors. The worst part about punishing him—or the best—was how Sunny reacted when he found out he had done something wrong. For example, one time Sunny hopped up on the green bench in the yard, where Peter had momentarily set his baseball glove while he went hunting a ball, and grabbed the glove in his mouth. By the time Peter found his dog and the glove, Sunny had already chewed through one of the finger holds.

Peter yelled in his boy-man voice, "Sunny? What in the world?"— imitating, without realizing it, the voice that I had used on Peter when he was a toddler. Sunny sank into the ground, like a cake falling when removed from the oven—completely deflated. His ears went down, his smiling doggie mouth trembled, his eyes looked to the side, and he began to slink along the ground away from Peter, casting tentative glances behind, as if we did not see him (for the girls and I had come out in the yard to witness the scene) and were not giggling uproariously behind our hands at his feeble attempts to cover up his crime.

He refused to look at Peter, no matter how many times Peter called his name. Instead, Sunny tried futilely to hide behind the bench. When Peter found him and approached him, Sunny rolled over on his back, legs dangling in the air. The doggie manual said that this was his self-defense. In complete surrender, on his back, with fear in his eyes, he was saying to Peter, "I'm sorry. Please don't hurt me, please."

Peter scolded his dog half-heartedly as Cara, Fran and I watched, laughter in our eyes.

"He's so hilarious," Cara said, in a rare moment of good humor. "It's like he thinks he can just disappear and get away with what he's done. He's a smart dog, but when he misbehaves, he sure acts stupid."

I stared at my daughter and didn't dare say a word. I wanted to say, Yes, dear, that sounds like someone else I know. But then I realized it wasn't just Cara who did the same thing when caught. So often I reacted in the same way as Sunny, slinking away from the Lord's presence, ignoring His gentle voice to come back. That day in our back yard I confessed to myself— and the Lord—that I had a very hard time admitting my guilt and asking for His forgiveness. Instead, I tended to hide or pout or make excuses and then, when the conviction was too strong, I would roll over and say, too quickly and without remorse, "Sorry, God! Please forgive me," hoping to escape the consequences.

I decided that day that Sunny wasn't the only one who needed obedience lessons. I could use a few lessons, too.

Chapter 11

One afternoon in autumn, when the leaves had started gliding off the trees and the air was brisk and fresh, the Good Woman drove me and My Boy out into the country. I sat on the back seat with my nose sticking out of the window and the breeze carrying a hundred different scents. Somewhere was honeysuckle and the last of the wild blackberries—which I actually like—and the odor of dying leaves and of freshly cut hay. We arrived at an open field where other cars were parked. A house sat off to the back and, on the right, there was a fenced-in area. I jumped up, placing my paws on the window, wiggling my body with excitement. I smelled dogs! Many, many dogs—males and females—right there in front of me. I barked to let them know I had arrived. I could not wait to get out of the car and begin to mark my territory.

When My Boy opened the door, I bounded out, yapping and straining on a Leash that was attached to a type of link-chain collar. It actually choked me if I pulled too hard. Still, the prospect of meeting other dogs overtook me, and I yanked all the harder.

This place seemed like the perfect playground. Dogs and humans and no Cages! Just wide, wooden fences that any dog could escape from and go dashing out into the countryside, chasing rabbits and birds. The only problem was that all of us had to stay on the Leash.

My Boy held the other end of the Leash, but he wasn't exactly prepared for my excitement. I rushed to the fence and barked hello to the other dogs—there were probably about a dozen of them, some just puppies. A few responded when I barked, but that caused their Master or Mistress to tug sharply on the Leash. Amazingly, this made them quiet down. All of us were wearing the same kind of collar around our necks and a hard yank on that collar made you think twice about barking again.

I must say that, although I got very excited seeing other dogs, I also felt extremely fearful of the males. Memories of the Cage and the other dogs jumping on me and threatening me and nipping at me rushed back as soon as I caught the scent of another male. I think I scared the humans with the way I rushed at other dogs, teeth bared and barking ferociously. But I had to do this to protect myself and to protect My Humans. They never really seemed to understand. I wished they could see that these reactions were for all of our good.

Inside the fence, there was a Strong Man in charge, teaching the humans and their dogs. He had long hair, and he was tall and stocky, exactly the kind of man who made me afraid. My Boy took me inside the fence where I joined the other dogs with a joyous yelp. "Shhh!" he said and yanked at me to no avail.

The Strong Man came over to us and took the Leash. My Boy stood off to the side of the big fenced-in corral with the Good Woman and watched as the Strong Man led me around.

I did not like that man! Whenever he yelled 'Heel'—which meant absolutely nothing to me at the time—he would yank the Leash with such force that he literally lifted me off the ground and swung me in an arc, strangling me. Any dog would be furious with this treatment. I certainly was. He was not my Master. I wanted to be in charge. So I let him know in the best way I could that I was not at all happy with him. I lifted my leg, and I peed on his jeans.

He noticed, but instead of letting me have my way, he yanked all the harder and yelled 'Heel' again and again. I peed on him three more times before I finally gave in and walked right by his side. I decided it was worth giving in—for the sake of my poor, sore neck. As soon as I obeyed, he reached down and petted me and said 'Good Dog' over and over.

I realized then that the Strong Man was also a good man who was simply trying to teach me. One thing that came easily for me was that I could learn. In fact, I liked learning things from the humans. I especially liked the way they praised me when I accomplished some task. Dogs like to make humans happy.

And so, to make them happy, I learned what the humans meant when they said, "Heel", "Come", "Stay", "Beg", "Sit", "Dance" and "Speak". And "Good Dog". I liked hearing "Good Dog" because that usually meant I would get something to eat. My Humans didn't seem to realize that I was constantly hungry. Whenever they gave me a chance to be a 'Good Dog'—by obeying one of those other commands—I took it. A dog will do anything to get food!

I went to that place in the country pretty often with the Good Woman and Peter. The most important thing I learned in the country was this: humans liked it when dogs obey. Most of the time, that wasn't hard at all for me to do.

I also learned the names of my humans. The Good Woman had several names. The children called her 'Mom', but when other people came to the house, they called her 'Lanie.' The Big Man simply called her 'Dear'. I liked that name for her best of all.

The Girls were 'Cara' and 'Fran' and the Big Man was 'Dad' or 'Hudson' or 'Sweetheart.'

But the best name of all was what they called My Boy. 'Peter'. I liked that name. I liked the sound, the rhythm, the cadence. Peter. My Peter.

I had a name, too. Often they called me 'Good Dog' and occasionally 'Bad Dog', but my favorite name was when Peter sat down beside me and stroked my fur and called me 'Sunny'.

Chapter 12

After almost two and a half months with Sunny, we decided that Peter was right. The dog needed to go to obedience school. He certainly was not like the dogs we jealously watched who walked calmly beside their owners without a leash. Sunny might have been mistreated and fearful, but as soon as he encountered another male dog, he tried to attack it. Twice, he had been successful, while on his leash. Even without the presence of other dogs, he strained on the leash, yanking and pulling and being completely disobedient.

So on a bright day in October with a slight breeze in the air, we drove to the obedience school. The instructor, an aging man named Hank, deeply tanned from a life spent outdoors and with the wisdom and love of animals etched in his face, explained the principle of getting a dog to heel. A dozen other pairs of owners and dogs immediately went about their work. Since it was our first day, the instructor offered to take Sunny and demonstrate how to teach him. We watched as Hank patiently, with silent power, held Sunny in, over and over again, forcing him to heel. Ultimately Sunny understood and obeyed, but not before he had sprayed the old man three times to show him, I think, how annoyed and offended he was.

When Hank returned Sunny to us, I apologized for the bad manners of our dog. The man smiled and said, "It's not the first time that has happened. But you need to realize, ma'am, that you have an extremely dominant dog."

By his third lesson at obedience school, Sunny had learned to 'heel', 'sit', 'stay' and 'come'. Amazingly, Peter unleashed him beside six other dogs, said "Stay" and walked to the other side of the corral. Peter stopped, turned to look at Sunny and the dog didn't budge. Then Peter pronounced one word, "Come", and Sunny bounded across the corral, paying no intention to other dogs, intent on joining his master.

Sunny also learned to sit patiently, muzzle in the air, while Peter filled a bowl with freshly ground beef and placed it smack dab in front of him. The dog didn't so much as flinch. I was impressed. Obedience school seemed to be working. In addition, Peter taught him to 'shake', 'beg', 'roll over' and 'dance'. Sunny also seemed to understand that it was a no-no to attack another dog, no matter what his instincts said. When he obeyed Peter's simple commands, Sunny was rewarded with a "Good dog!" and a treat. He wagged his tail; he seemed thrilled to have pleased his master. This was great progress.

And so I started bringing Sunny to the park down the street from our house on afternoons when I returned from the library before Peter came home from school. We had learned from Hank that a dominant male on a leash would naturally act aggressive when approached by a free-running male because the leashed dog felt that his territory was being threatened. Hank was right. Sunny lunged on the leash toward the other dogs which were running free. Other owners urged me to let him loose. I hesitated. Yes, Sunny had stopped attacking other males at obedience school, but I wasn't so sure about his reactions in the park. But amazingly, the moment I slipped the chain off his neck, he took off at break-neck speed, galloping and frolicking with his new friends.

The park became a place for Sunny to learn freedom and fun and obedience, and a place for him to meet friends. It took a while for him to gain my trust, but gradually (after he had attacked several dogs and been severely scolded) I let him off the leash as soon as I got to the park, and for the next thirty minutes, Sunny galloped to his heart's content through tall grass. Heaven had come to earth for Sunny. One of my favorite memories is of that first autumn, with the leaves in their burnt-copper shades and the burnt-copper mutt running beneath the trees, at full speed, almost parallel to the ground, a red blur weaving his way through the grass.

Hank had told us we had a smart dog. At the park, I learned that we had a fast dog, a very fast dog. In the years to come, I would always be thankful for that.

Chapter 13

The Good Woman liked to paint.

In the mornings, all of My Humans left me alone at the house. Usually I stayed outside in the fenced-in back yard where I could run in the grass and watch squirrels in the pear tree. I was never allowed in the front yard, except when My Boy was with me. A long driveway ran from the street all the way to the back yard. A wire gate which was attached to the wire fence divided the driveway into the front and back yards. At the end of the driveway in the back was an opened garage where the humans kept their car and also stored all kinds of things— such as the Good Woman's paints. Whenever I heard the sound of a car passing by, I would rush to the wire gate, bark and watch and wait.

In the middle of the day, the Good Woman drove the car into the driveway, opened the wire gate, shooed me out of the way and pulled the car into the garage. I always got excited when she came home, because that meant she was going to take me for a walk in the park! When we returned from our walk, she sat down on the couch in the den with her big book and read it for a while. Sometimes she talked out loud, but I could tell that she was not talking to me.

Then she went outside to the garage and got out her paints. I liked it when she took out the paints. I liked that smell, a mixture of acid and oil and newness. She used little brushes which she dipped in different colors and then transferred to a big white board. Little by little the board filled with colors.

But one day, she decided to paint a Bench. It was an old Bench that the Big Man had found beside the road—I know because I was with him—and the Big Man put new wood on places where the wood was rotted and then the Good Woman painted it a dark color. She hummed and sang while she painted. She was happy. She would not let me get near the Bench for a long time. I wanted to obey her, but that lovely scent of new and acid kept enticing me.

When the phone rang and she answered it (humans like to talk loud into this contraption—even though there is no one else around.

At least they pick it up so that it stops that awful ringing that hurts my ears), I went into the garage and sniffed the Bench. I was just lifting my leg to mark it so that everyone would know it was My Bench, when the Good Woman hurried into the garage and cried, "Stop!" She grabbed me by the collar and led me into the house. Later the Bench would be in the yard and I would spray it with my urine. But that day, I just obeyed and stayed in the house, trying hard to lick off some strange substance that had adhered itself to my fur. Funny thing. It smelled a lot like that Bench.

Chapter 14

Sometimes I think my heart is so very hard. Sometimes it feels stiff, like muscles that haven't been used in a while. But sometimes, Lord, it breaks. It breaks in that way that means it is really pumping. It's not always a wrenching, horrible thing that breaks my heart. Often it is the simplest of scenes or a sudden memory that makes it start hurting somewhere deep inside. A good kind of ache, like when those stiff, unused muscles have had a good workout and afterwards are sore.

What was it that touched my heart during that first year that Sunny was with us? It was looking out the big windows in the den to the little back yard and seeing that beautiful mutt curled up asleep on the green bench that was never really meant for him. My tears welled up and I smiled. That crazy, loveable mutt had brought such joy into our lives. He had wreaked pandemonium and ruined rugs and shoes and worn down the grass in the yard. He had even streaked himself with green paint that I finally had to cut out of his fur.

But it was worth it, putting up with his antics.

That was why I smiled through tears, seeing him uncharacteristically sprawled out on the bench. Usually he was dashing madly about the little, fenced-in yard. But that day he was asleep and so peaceful. Rescued from what we called 'the pit of hell', he had found a home where he was certainly loved. He was indeed part of the family.

It also touched my heart to see Peter when he was in one of his angry, silent moods (which seemed to happen more and more often) go into the garage and love on Sunny. He buried his face in his rust-colored fur and talked sweetly to him, and the anger dissipated. I learned from Sunny that sometimes the best thing I could do for Peter was just to be there, not saying a word, and allow him to be angry or sad.

It touched my heart to watch Peter work out his endless energy in wrestling matches with his dog. Most of his sweatshirts and many of his T-shirts had holes in them by the time Sunny had been with us for a few months, but who cared? A boy and his dog!

I also got that aching as I observed Sunny waiting for Peter to come home from school. It was the way he waited—with his ears. Sunny had so many ways to express his emotions, but especially with his ears. Human ears just don't move the way dogs do. He'd be lying peacefully in the back yard dozing. Then he must have heard something. I certainly hadn't. But suddenly he was aware, at attention, still lying with his belly on the cement, but now his ears were pricked forward. He tilted his head and his eyes came alive with expression. He sat up, ears going up and down. Then he was on his feet, tail beginning to wag and then as he stood with his ears pricked, he looked to the street in that bright, expectant way and broke into a run toward the wire gate. Sometimes the dog seemed more like a colt, frolicking and galloping, his hindquarters gathered under him as he leapt in a smooth up and down rhythm. As soon as Peter opened the gate, Sunny jumped up, paws on Peter's chest, greeting him with a sharp yelp of joy, and I heard the amazing sound of crackling laughter coming from my son. I observed this from afar. I just watched and wiped tears from my eyes because it touched my heart.

One day as I watched that scene, I came to the conclusion that I wanted to greet My Lord in the same way that Sunny greeted Peter—waiting expectantly, listening for His presence, and running joyfully into His arms.

Chapter 15

I had been with My Humans for a good while. Snow had come and gone, the trees had given off their fragrance of blossoms and then fruit, the grass had turned green and then almost brown under the hot, hot sun. Eventually Peter and Cara and Fran did not leave early in the mornings. Instead, I waited and waited for My Boy to come downstairs. I was not allowed to go up the steps, although several times, when the Humans left me alone in the house, I sneaked up there just to have a look.

But My Boy took a long time to come downstairs in the morning. Waiting was worth it, because after he ate his food, he went outside with me, before the sun got too hot, and we played ball. Again and again and again I chased the tennis ball or the baseball and brought it to him.

The humans protected My Boy because he limped. I didn't know why, what had happened. Perhaps he had had a Worst Day of All like I had. I only knew that he was slower moving than other kids his age and that made him afraid. I smelled the fear on him. The Girls, Cara and Fran, invited friends over often—other humans their age with whom they played. But My Boy rarely had friends over.

The Good Woman worried about My Boy. I smelled the worry as I smelled the fear. She watched him from afar. She didn't speak to him very often, but she watched. Sometimes after My Boy spent time with me, the Good Woman looked relieved. I wished I could tell her that she did not need to worry about My Boy. He would never hurt me. And his heart was strong. And I would always protect him. He rescued me. I would never leave him. Ever.

One day in the hot summer, My Boy put me on the Leash and stuck a backpack on his back. An adventure! My Boy had stuffed his backpack with food. I could smell the beef and the bread and the tuna and other wonderful things which normally I was not allowed to eat, but which I knew I would get when I was alone with Peter. We shared everything.

I hopped in the back of the car. That was always my spot when Peter whistled to me and called, "Come on, Sunny!" and he hit the side of the car. I leapt into the opened trunk, yelping in my happy way and wagging my tail. What could be better than a car ride with My Boy? The Good Woman and the Big Man got in the front seat of the car. The Big Man drove and My Boy sat in the back and leaned over the seat and petted me. He was always careful to make sure I wasn't afraid. Of course, I wasn't afraid. I was with him!

On this day, we drove for a long time, and then the Big Man parked the car in the shade of tall trees. My Boy bounded out of the back seat, opened the trunk and called, "Come on, Sunny!" and I leapt out, ecstatic. The Good Woman looked worried again but the Big Man held her and smiled and waved to us and told My Boy something and then they drove off. I wagged my tail as I watched them go, the Good Woman looking back over her shoulder with that liquid running down her face.

Chapter 16

Almost a year after Sunny came to live with us, Peter insisted on taking him camping, the two of them, alone on the Appalachian Trail for one night and two days. We were shocked at this suggestion. Our son? The son who cowered in PE class wanted to camp on the Trail alone with his dog?

"This will be a good experience—a boy and his dog. Don't worry. You worry too much, Lanie," Hudson said.

But he knew I had a good reason to worry. Peter didn't use to cower in PE. He had friends, many friends, before the accident. Hudson and I had talked through this many times. Peter was a devoted Boy Scout and a fairly decent athlete. He played soccer, and he loved to go camping with his dad and friends.

I cannot write the rest without my heart in my throat.

The accident happened on a camping trip on the Appalachian Trail.

Hudson had a tradition of taking each of our children on a special trip for his or her tenth birthday. With Cara they went out west to a dude ranch and rode horses. With Fran, she chose a ski trip to Colorado.

Peter chose camping along the Appalachian Trail with his father, his best friend, Matthew, and Matthew's dad, Mike. Five days on the trail, complete with hiking, canoeing and rock climbing. A perfect outing, a perfect way for Hudson and his son to celebrate Peter's tenth birthday, even if it came nearer to his eleventh one.

What do you say about a freak accident? A canoe that tipped over. A boy's foot that got caught in the rocks underwater. Another boy who dove down to free his friend's leg and struck his head on a rock and was knocked unconscious. A father who went after his unconscious boy and another who stayed to free his son, who had to break the leg, a terrible break, to dislodge it. The boy who screamed in pain, the father who dragged him to shore and left him there and went after the other father to search for the unconscious son. The boy who lay there in excruciating pain for an hour or more while the fathers searched and searched and searched for his friend. The night that fell and the medics who came to take the injured boy away to the hospital and the father torn between going with his son or continuing with his friend and the forest rangers on a futile search.

What do you say?

In the end, Peter was flown to County General here in our town. The break to his leg was so bad that it had to be reset three times. It eventually healed, but for years afterwards, Peter had a pronounced limp.

Matthew's body was found by a fisherman a week later much further down the river.

Who can recover from tragedy? A hundred questions asked. Why was our son spared and Matthew taken? A long, low, moaning why that stuck in our throats and froze us with its silence.

And Peter, mute and sullen, asked his own questions over and over and over again in his head. Why did I want to go camping? How did I let the canoe overturn? How did my foot get stuck? Why did Matthew have to dive in to the river? Why did he strike his head on a rock?

They were questions without answers, but what I knew, the answer I did have, was that after that horrible event, Peter was never the same.

Then Sunny came to our home, and we felt a stirring of hope.

I watched my husband watch his son as Peter and Sunny walked off onto the trail, the same trail he had taken two years ago, with Hudson and Matthew and Mike. We had to let him go, a thirteen-year-old with a limp, a boy who needed to live again, needed adventure, needed to know that we trusted him and needed to prove that he could move on.

I watched them go with tears streaming down my face.

In that moment, Sunny became much more than the sweet and slightly neurotic dog we had rescued from the Humane Society. I mentally transferred a huge weight of responsibility to that mutt. Sunny would protect my son. He had to.

I prayed to the Lord and cleared my throat, and I almost leaned out the window and called out, "Please don't go near the river." Instead, we waved again, and I made my voice light, even though tears were blurring my vision. I forced the tears away, and I opened my mouth and said, "Have fun."

Chapter 17

A dog cannot be much happier than alone in the woods with His Boy. I trotted beside Peter, occasionally licking his hand, then bounding ahead to chase a squirrel and mark yet another tree as my own. It was simply my way of saying, "I've been here, guys, so watch out! Stay away!" My Boy at times grew impatient of my many halts to spray a bush or plant.

Humans just have a hard time understanding the importance of urine.

We hiked along a beautiful trail with odors that wafted at me from every direction—wild smells, free smells of dying leaves and thick bark on the trees and bushes calling out from everywhere to be marked as my own.

There were other smells that made me wary. Smells of animals I did not recognize, smells of mothers with their young. We occasionally met other humans on the trail, and once in a while a dog, but the more likely inhabitants were an array of different birds and butterflies and lizards, baking on a rock in the sun. Once in a while Peter let me chase a plump gray squirrel until it scurried up a tree while I barked, begging it to come down. Not one squirrel ever listened to me.

My Boy seemed to know exactly where he was heading, but after several hours of hiking, he was tired. I could tell because the limp was more pronounced, and he slowed his pace quite a bit. So I lay down in the shade of a tree while he leaned his back against the trunk, and we drank water and nibbled food and rested.

I was surprised to see that My Boy knew how to do things, many things, like put up a tent and start a fire with just sticks and stones and a match that flared in the night. I saw a confidence in his eyes that I had never seen during the time we had been together, and this made me wag my tail and lick his arms in that way that gave him the little-boy giggles.

During the night of camping, I was asleep in the tent, cuddled up beside My Boy—he had wrapped himself in a sleeping bag—when I was awakened by a Sound. This Sound was close by and the smell let me know it was one of those animals I had never met before, but one Mother had told me about long ago, an enormous animal made fierce because of her young. I jumped to my feet and began to whine. I did not like the smell of this animal. It smelled like anger and danger. I whined again and licked My Boy, and he finally roused. He petted me, and I could tell he wanted to go back to sleep, so I nudged him with my muzzle and then pushed him and whined again.

He asked me a question and then grabbed his flashlight and went to the tent flap and peered into the dark. Now I was barking, warning him. The animal was near, very near and mad. I can smell anger.

I rushed out into the night and found a big black animal—what humans call a Bear—standing on her hind legs and trying to knock down the backpack which My Boy had hung up high on a limb of a tree. When the Bear saw me, she growled, her white fangs shining in the night. A cub, about my size, huddled near her. I braced my legs and showed my fangs and my hair stood up on my spine. I barked at My Boy and told him to find cover. But Humans never really understand what I am trying to tell them.

Now My Boy was afraid, and he did not know what to do. I smelled terror on him. He was calling to me, trying to tell me something. "Stay! Stay, Sunny!" He repeated over and over. But I would not stay and let the black mother Bear run after him. He was afraid for himself but he was more afraid for me, and I loved him even more for this.

The mother Bear growled, standing up on her haunches and batting the air with her huge paws. Finally she knocked the backpack off the tree limb. It fell to the ground beside me. I knew what I had to do. I grabbed the strap of the backpack in my mouth and dragged it beside me as I ran. It was no longer heavy for we had consumed most of its contents in our first day of camping. I knew that the Bear wanted the food inside. She was not after My Boy. I heard her growl again and then the sound of her heavy body loping after me.

My Boy began climbing up a tree, slowly, in the dark, screaming at me, and I ran, holding that strap in my mouth and pulling it along behind me, far away from My Boy. I heard the Bear crashing through the woods, gaining on me. In another moment, she would have pounced on me, devouring me and the contents of the backpack. But I dropped the bag, and I kept running. She did not follow. Instead, the Bear stopped. I continued to run further into the woods.

Later, I returned to where I had dropped the backpack. I saw where the Bear had ripped it open with one huge paw. She had found the food, devoured it—or perhaps given it to her cub—and then walked away. I followed her scent, relieved to find that she had gone in the opposite direction of where I had left My Boy. I waited and watched, but the Bear and her cub did not return. I took the backpack in my teeth and pulled it along beside me as I retraced my path back to My Boy.

There he was, still up in the tree. When he saw me coming, he screamed for joy, jumped down from his perch and hugged me tightly. He was crying. I could feel the liquid from his eyes on my fur.

But he was safe. I had done my job. I had protected My Boy.

Chapter 18

Can tragedy strike twice in the same spot? All I know is that after we picked up Peter and Sunny—and the shredded backpack—at the arranged spot, and Peter related their adventure in vivid details, describing the scene from his position on a tree branch, there was a soft confidence in his voice. This time, would-be tragedy had turned into triumph. Again and again, Peter told of the way Sunny woke him in the night and of the hungry black bear that growled and stood on her haunches, trying to get the backpack, of how he scraped his legs raw, shimming up that scrawny pine tree and how he feared the branch would snap under his weight. Peter's favorite part of the story was describing the bear dislodging the backpack and of Sunny grabbing it, before the bear could react, and carrying it far away.

"He was protecting me, Mom. Every step of the way. Sunny did it. He ran fast. He made the bear chase him. Sunny saved my life."

Together, boy and dog had outsmarted the mother bear.

I do not know what would have happened to my son if the bear had gotten his dog. I cannot contemplate this. I only know that I thanked God that our loyal mutt was also a fast mutt and a smart mutt.

And I know that Peter returned from that experience more of a man, more confident, more determined. The fire that had been in the old Peter's eyes returned too. And I truly think that he limped less. He became almost fiercely protective of his dog, and he would not let me throw the torn backpack out. For years and years it hung on a nail on the wall of Peter's room. I think he kept it there to remind him that some near-tragedies turn out okay. Or maybe he just kept it as proof of how his dog saved his life.

I decided that this new confidence came from Peter and Sunny being a team, a very good team.

Chapter 19

There are images that stay in a mother's mind forever. Some of my favorite ones come from when Peter turned fifteen. With a shy confidence about him, he let his hair grow longer, so that it curled softly on the ends as it hung below his ears. Hudson and I figured that if this was an act of defiance, it was a very small one, and we never said a word. A sweet girl from the church youth group hung around Peter a lot, but honestly, he seemed oblivious, even after both Cara and Fran spelled it out clearly. "She has a crush on you, Pete. You should ask her out."

Peter never did, probably because 'asking someone out' in our family meant that you could invite the date to our house for dinner. Period. No other options until the child turned seventeen.

But I liked Peter's fifteenth year because he began to discover his passions in a new way, and I guess it was the last year where Sunny was his sole companion. In the years to follow, Peter gained friends, many friends. He still made time for his dog, still wrestled with him and went on walks with him. I would still find him curled up near Sunny's bed, pouring out his heart to the mutt—especially after that sweet girl from the youth group broke Peter's seventeen-year-old heart.

But at fifteen, Peter's heart was still all and only for Sunny.

Fifteen was the age when Peter gave great, awkward smiles and didn't care at all what clothes he wore, much to the horror of his sisters who swore he was a disgrace to the family with his jeans hanging off his bottom so that the whole world could see his very un-cool underwear.

At fifteen, Peter didn't care.

He played soccer again, defense, with all the passion of a professional, and I became a 'soccer mom', yelling from the stands as his blond hair flopped in his eyes and on his shoulders.

That was the year that Peter and Sunny started jogging together daily. When they returned, Peter was covered in sweat, soaked and panting almost as hard as the dog. "Pulled me along up 'Heartbreak Hill'," he puffed out, leaning over and heaving. "Wouldn't have made it without Sunny yanking me along on the last mile."

Fifteen was endless energy and unconditional love for his dog. And honestly, it was enough. When on occasion his unbridled energy spilled over to humans, and he hugged me in a moment of pure abandon, I felt like hopping on the kitchen counter and doing a tap dance around the bread crumbs and little piles of grape jelly and peanut butter, left there by a hungry and hurried adolescent.

I am a sentimental mother, and I did not want that fifteenth year to end.

Do mothers have premonitions? Is it intuition? Perhaps. All I know is that both Sunny and I sensed that change was around the corner, blowing in the wind, and when Sunny lifted his muzzle to smell it, I blinked back tears.

Chapter 20

Peter was invited by four friends to go camping out west for a month the summer after his sophomore year in high school. Although he had enjoyed Boy Scout camp as a young boy, after the accident, Peter never showed any interest in camping with anyone except his dog. The plain truth was that Peter did not want to leave Sunny. Period.

Then he turned sixteen, made a few good friends and began planning this 'Out West' trip with them. One day, Peter asked me—with tears in his eyes—how he could explain to Sunny that he was going away for a while.

"Do you think he knows that I'm leaving? Can he tell, Mom? I certainly don't want him to think that I'm leaving him forever."

Peter agonized over the fact that he could not explain to his dog that he would be absent for a month. The night before Peter left, he sat on the floor beside Sunny's bed and petted him for hours. He didn't know that he was humming a tune, did not know that he spoke his thoughts out loud.

"I'll be back. I promise. It won't be long. I'll come back. You just try to be good, fella. Do what Mom says. Don't make her nervous or mad, okay? She'll feed you, and she'll take you on long walks, if you remember to heel."

He talked on and on to his dog, reassuring him, humming, singing. He fell asleep on the floor downstairs beside Sunny. I guess Peter woke up sometime in the night and went upstairs, because the next morning I had to rouse him from his own bed. The first thing he did was run downstairs and call for Sunny. And, as always, Sunny met him with an eager wag of the tail and then he leaped up, planting his front legs on Peter's thighs. Next Sunny collapsed on the floor, rolling onto his back with those big red ears falling open, lifting one paw into the air and waiting patiently for Peter to get the same hint he gave every morn. This is my stomach and I'd like you to scratch it. Of course Peter obeyed.

In fact, I often wondered who had really gone to obedience

E L I Z A B E T H   M U S S E R

school—the dog or the boy. Or maybe they had simply learned together, which seemed to me a very fitting way for things to be for a boy and his dog.

As I watched them there that morning before Peter left, I got the cramping in my heart that always came when the Lord was nudging me. Once again I compared myself to Sunny and wondered if I could sit still long enough—without doing anything—to find great joy and warmth and contentment beside my Master. I wondered if I dared to lift myself up to Him and ask Him to soothe me, just because I knew he loved me and wanted to bring me pleasure. No matter how much I knew of my Savior and Lord, I think I still expected Him to be disappointed with me. I couldn't quite imagine that it was okay with Him for me to spend time with him, down on the floor, huddled under the stairs, safe and comfortable and never wanting to leave.

Chapter 21

I sensed that something odd was about to happen. My Boy seemed excited and nervous and preoccupied. I smelled sadness and happiness mixed together. We still took our romps and jogs and wrestled out in the back yard with the sun beating down on us. He stayed close to me, but his eyes betrayed something. I tried to understand. I sat still, head up, tail thumping slowly, looking dignified while he hugged my neck. I pricked my ears to hear what was different. I listened and smelled and watched. If I had known he was leaving, I think I would have sniffed him longer, letting his boy-man scent fill up every part of me so that I would not forget him.

Early one morning, Peter bounded down the stairs, carrying a stuffed back pack. He set it down at the foot of the stairs, near where I slept. The sleeping bag we used on adventures lay there too. And food. I smelled food. I circled these things with excitement. Another trip with My Boy!

When I wagged my tail and nudged him with my muzzle, he knelt down beside me, looked me in the eyes and said, "Stay, Sunny. Stay." I did not understand why he said this when he was obviously going on an adventure. We always went on adventures together.

A car full of big boys, loud, smelly, laughing boys, came into the driveway. They patted me in a distracted way when Peter introduced me. I could tell they were eager to be on their way to this adventure. I barked and dashed around the yard. An adventure with My Boy and his friends!

My Boy lifted his bag into the trunk of the car, and I rushed after him and leapt inside. I knew my place in the car. I lay down contentedly between other backpacks and sleeping bags. One boy laughed, but the others were not smiling at me. They said something to Peter. He gave them a shrug and his fake smile, the one he gave his parents when they asked him too many questions. He came to the trunk and gave me a pat and I looked up at him, licked his hand and let my tail thump slowly on the bottom of the trunk. I did not like the way he was looking at me. Thump, thump, thump.

"No, Sunny," he said in a cracking voice. I could tell he didn't mean it, so I licked him again and gave a little yelp. "No," he repeated and then he reached for my collar and pulled on it. I pulled back, thinking he was playing. This time, he gave a yank, more forcefully than every before.

"Sunny!" he said, and I heard the exasperation in his voice. I had heard that sound in the voice of the Big Man and the Good Woman, but never in My Boy's voice. I stood up slowly, hopped out of the trunk and slinked away.

I don't think he noticed. Peter got in the car with the others, and one of the boys started the motor and began to back the car out.

I stood in the driveway with my head up and watched him leave. He waved to me and then he was gone.

Day after day I waited for him to come home, but he did not. He was not there in the mornings to greet me as he stumbled down the stairs. He did not appear in the driveway in the afternoons and he did not eat with the Big Man, the Good Woman and the Girls at dinner.

Why would My Boy leave me? What did it mean? I wanted to know that he was well. I wanted him to know that I missed him and that I was trying to obey the Big Man and the Good Woman. There were other people who came, other humans who took care of me, but no one did it like My Boy. Would I ever see him again?

Sometimes I grew afraid that I would forget his particular smell and the sound of his voice. Once I rushed into the den, barking at the odor I had caught in the air, and I expected to find him standing there. But there was only his baseball glove, lying on the couch. Another time, the Good Woman left me at home inside and I sneaked upstairs to his room. His smell was all around me; I felt his presence. I jumped on his bed and waited, hoping that soon he would come. Even if he didn't come, I would be there; I would wait.

Chapter 22

The wait was long for Sunny on Peter's first trip away. Whenever the doorbell rang, Sunny hopped across the back yard, ears up, a brightness in his rusty eyes. Such eagerness, such hope.

"I think he's waiting for Peter," I told Hudson one day.

It struck me as I said it—did I wait for my Lord like that? No—most of the time I was so busy, so rushed, that I barely had time to find my Bible. I couldn't wait. I needed God to show up and fast, before the next appointment.

Sunny waited.

Sunny also went on a hunger strike. The third day after Peter left, when Sunny figured out that his boy was not going to come down the stairs, he sat down and waited. And waited. Then he refused to eat. His food sat untouched in his bowl. I tried to coax him, sat down beside him and held out a handful of the croquettes. Sunny didn't even look at me. He kept his head high, staring far away, as if he were back at obedience school and he was not allowed to notice the food.

I grew worried. "Is he mad at us? Mad at Peter?"

Hudson thought about this for a moment. "I think he doesn't trust us any more. I think he's afraid we'll all leave and not come back."

I started eating my breakfast outside on the bench, with Sunny's bowl on the ground beside me. And gradually he came over and began to eat his food, warily watching to make sure I didn't move. I marveled at Sunny's determination. I knew that dogs were loyal, but I had never heard of one going on a hunger strike. Needless to say, I was relieved when he began to eat again.

Inevitably as I watched our mutt sitting patiently in the driveway, I went out to him. I scratched behind his ears, the way he liked it. I brushed his rust coat with a wide-pronged comb. I even sneaked him a leftover piece of steak as I whispered, "I'll wait here with you, Sunny. I know it's hard."

There was a catch in my throat when I said it. Why, I wondered? I guess it was because I knew that pretty soon I'd be like Sunny, waiting and not knowing exactly when the next time would be that I'd see this son. Already it was that way with our girls. Cara was off at college, and Fran was so busy with her senior year, she hardly knew where her bed was any more.

At least boys come home when they're hungry, I thought, trying to console myself.

At that moment, I knew what Sunny did not, could not, know. In three and a half weeks, Peter would return with a backpack filled with dirty laundry and a month full of living legends to share.

That made my wait easier.

But someday in the not-too-distant future, Sunny and I would wait together, alone, keeping each other company. Someday, my nest would be empty.

It was hard to wait alone. Alone, our minds rushed to the worst possible scenario, we grew weary, and we worried. God knew this, and so, often as we were waiting on something from the Lord, in the midst of the craziness of life, He sent a fellow traveler along to encourage us and wait by our sides—as I was now waiting with Sunny. That made the whole process more bearable.

Sitting on the front porch of our house, my arms draped around Sunny's neck, I let memories sketch themselves in my mind. Clutching the hands of my dear friends as I waited to hear news of Peter's accident. Sobbing on the couch at another friend's home as I spilled out my terror at Peter's depression. Grabbing my friend in a death hug as she wailed the loss of her son. Hudson looking me in the eyes, holding my face tenderly in his hands and saying, "We are going to make it, together, one day at a time."

I buried my face in Sunny's soft coat, squeezed him harder, thankful that between us, no words were necessary. He sat there, always dignified, some kind of wisdom in his eyes. I wondered what he saw, what he understood. I wished I could get into his doggie mind and see how he was processing Peter's disappearance.

As I watched our mutt, I leaned into the squeezing in my heart, that in-between type of pain, and I whispered out loud, "Lord, I want to wait for You in the same way Sunny waits for Peter. Ears up, head erect, expectantly. At any moment now, he is sure his Master is going to come to him. And he is ready."

Chapter 23

I was curled up on the Bench in the back yard, dozing and occasionally lifting my head to stare at the blue jay in the little pear tree, when I heard it. The sound of a car coming in the driveway and then the sound of a car door opening and shutting. I lifted my head, tilted it a little and thought I heard something else. A voice. His voice. I sprang off the Bench and hurried to the back door, whining and pawing it.

"Sunny! Sunny!" It was his voice.

The back door opened and he attacked me in a hug and we were rolling in the grass and I was licking his face and wagging my tail and planting my paws on his chest and he was laughing and laughing and laughing.

My Boy came back to me. It was worth the wait!

But after that first adventure without me, My Boy went away more often. I could not predict when I would see him again. On many days he still stumbled down the steps and found me at the bottom and rubbed my stomach in that affectionate way. But he did not seem to have as much time for me. I brought my favorite old chewed-up baseball to him, dropping it at his feet, but he did not pick it up and toss it in the yard for me to fetch. My Boy was preoccupied by other things. Even when he petted me, he seemed busy in his mind. Humans do not have the ability to express things with their ears, but I could tell he was thinking, maybe worrying, maybe sad, by the inflection in his voice and the way he moved, slowly, concentrating.

I moved that way when I saw a squirrel or a blue jay. I froze and stared and pointed. I prepared myself to leap at the unsuspecting animal. My Boy did this in a different way. His eyes were intense; he seemed distracted, as if he could not afford to play with his dog because other things were very important.

He now drove that contraption that humans called a car. He brought friends home with him. Male and female. The girls always made a fuss over me. "Beautiful dog," they said. They petted me and brushed me. The boys played with me, throwing balls and watching me run. Sometimes, Peter's friends spent the night at the house, four or five of them stretched across the den in their sleeping bags. When I sensed one of them was sad, I cuddled up beside him.

I liked My Boy's friends, but I missed the special times alone with My Boy, the way we played tug-of-war with the shirt or baseball I found in the yard, the way we ran together and I helped him along when he was too tired. I missed My Boy, and now I was never sure he would be there in the morning.

When he was gone too long, I stopped eating. If he knew I was hungry and waiting on him to eat, surely he would come back. That didn't work. The only thing it accomplished was to make the Good Woman worried, so worried that she sat with me and talked and begged me to eat from her hand. When she got her own food and sat down beside me, I relaxed and ate. She wasn't leaving. I gobbled down my food.

How I loved to find the smell of My Boy, even when he was far away. The Good Woman pretended she did not like these smells— of dirty socks and underwear, of sweat and caked mud and grass, of wadded-up candy wrappers in his jeans, of smelly old tennis shoes. But I think she liked them as much as I did, those special scents that were his, a mixture of leather gloves and bad breath, dried blood and sweat, potato chips and chocolate, all stirred together to make My Boy.

Chapter 24

Sunny had been with us for six years when I first noticed a bit of gray on his muzzle and flecks of white in the rust fur around his eyes. We estimated that he was seven years old which made him 49 in human years. When I realized this, I marveled that he and I were just about the same age. Not that Sunny was showing signs of slowing down. He still galloped madly around the back yard, dashing to the fence when the postman came to deliver the mail, yapping furiously as if he was warning me of imminent peril.

That was the year that Peter left for college, packing up the scattered contents of his room into our little hatchback. We prepared to drive him halfway across the country so that he could study some type of Animal Biology at a school in the Midwest. Peter had decided he wanted to be a vet.

Peter was going away—not to camp, not on vacation. He was going to college. How would he explain this to Sunny? It was hard enough for me to understand.

On the last day before he left, Peter took Sunny out for a jog. This had not happened in months. Peter had been preoccupied with everything that went into getting finished with high school and ready for college. I was happy to see him fasten the leash to Sunny's collar and then slip the other end around his waist where he hooked it. Those obedience lessons from years ago had paid off so that Peter could jog, hands free, with Sunny beside him.

They returned about half an hour later, Peter covered in sweat, Sunny's tongue hanging out, his sides heaving in and out, in and out. Peter looked stricken. He unleashed his dog and Sunny kept pacing back and forth on the porch, a wild look in his eyes. He refused to lap the water from the bowl Peter placed in front of him. The dog sank to the ground, tongue playing a wet staccato rhythm. We both knelt down beside Sunny, but as soon as we began to pet him, he shook himself as if our touch was painful or at least bothersome. He struggled up and paced and paced.

"I don't know what's the matter with him, Mom," Peter said.

"Should I call the vet?"

"How was he on the jog?"

"He started out same as always, pulling me along. But after about twenty minutes, when we got to 'Heartbreak Hill', he started lagging behind—and then I almost had to pull him along. I teased him a little, until I realized he really couldn't keep up with me." A sob escaped from my eighteen-year-old son. His Adam's apple was bobbing up and down as he fought to control his emotions. "We finished the jog more slowly, didn't we, fella?" Peter scooped some water into his hands and held it out to the dog. Sunny lapped it up, then began pacing again.

"I think he's just getting older, sweetie," I offered.

Peter narrowed his eyes at me, as if daring me to say another word. He turned his full attention on his dog. Eventually Sunny's breathing returned to normal, he lapped more water and collapsed on the porch in a patch of sun. Peter sat there for a long time, stroking his dog, murmuring something to him. I busied myself getting the last load of Peter's clothes out of the dryer and calling Fran—who was living ten minutes away in a house with friends—to make sure she remembered she needed to feed Sunny while Hudson and I took Peter to college.

But I had a huge lump in my throat as I went about these tasks. Peter had grown so accustomed to his dog. His loyalty never faltered even if the time he could spend with Sunny had diminished. This day, my son had realized in a new way the mortality of his beast. I saw it in his eyes, and it scared me.

Sunny got a lot of credit for the way Peter went through high school, more confident, more willing to take on an opponent, with a mischievous gleam of hope in his eyes. I truly think that the jogging incident forced Peter, for the very first time, to say to himself, "My dog won't be around forever."

At midnight, the day before he left for college, Peter was still lying next to Sunny on that worn-out rug that reeked of dog. The thought struck me then—did Peter want to be a vet so that he could somehow miraculously make his dog immortal? I shivered at the thought, silly though it be.

Chapter 25

The day came when I could no longer keep up with Peter on a jog. Perhaps I couldn't keep up, but I would die trying. That is how we dogs are. Even humans know that dogs are loyal.

Some of my favorite times with My Boy had been our jogs together. When we first started running into the unknown, Peter had difficulty keeping up with me because he limped badly. But gradually, as we went out day after day after day, his limp improved. Peter also grew tall, almost as tall as the Big Man, even though he remained thin like a limb on the little pear tree in the back yard. Gradually, we ran together, in synch, hardly breaking a sweat up that steep, steep hill. As we ran, the odors of outdoors just washed over me, enticing me to pull ahead or lag behind. Occasionally My Boy let me stop and sniff as I marked my territory. We came back from those outings in nature panting and content. I could always tell when My Boy was truly happy.

After the incident with the Bear, My Boy became more confident, more determined, and he grew stronger so that the jogs covered more distance. In my mind, our countless jogs together were like a blissful blur, something every boy and dog should experience. I wiggled with excitement when My Boy came into the backyard, the Leash in hand, and bent down to ask me if I wanted to go on a jog with him. The inflection in his voice was always the same; his eyes gleamed in that teasing way I loved. Did I want to go? Yelp and yelp and yelp and yes, yes, yes! Wag, wag, wag.

Then one day when he took me out, I found I could no longer keep up with him. We had not gone for a jog together in a long time. I tried, I really tried hard. I don't think he could understand what was happening. My Boy was as fresh as the bread the Good Woman baked in her oven. But I was tired, and I found that the Leash fastened to my collar and around My Boy's waist grew taut as he pulled ahead. He slowed his pace and spoke soothing words to me. My Boy waited for me to catch up. But I felt shame and sadness. I could no longer keep up with My Boy! I was thankful to get home, but my heart would not stop racing and cramping. Instinct told me that I had to walk and walk and walk.

My Boy stayed with me that night, slept in my bed, just like long ago.

But I think I disappointed My Boy because the next day, he went away. They all went away in a car piled high with things humans need. I watched from the driveway behind that wire gate.

But I would wait for them, wait for him, until he came back. I had waited before. Perhaps he was disappointed, but I knew My Boy. He loved me. He knew I would never let him down.

Chapter 26

Bittersweet was that homecoming after leaving Peter at college. My days were mixed with tears and laughter, knowing and questioning, energy and fatigue. I stood on the porch and looked out at the green lawn with a hint of autumn in the air and drops from a recent rain on the trees. I vacuumed and scrubbed the house, dusting and cleaning and straightening and preparing to jump back into my work at the library.

And so I did.

But my heart was heavy, missing Peter and then missing the girls all over again. I thought by the third time, I would have gotten used to this routine of packing them up and leaving them at school and knowing this was exactly as it should be. Perhaps I was used to it, but it didn't feel any easier. I heard Peter's voice over the phone sounding fragile and, perhaps, a little lonely. I felt alone, too, as if no one else could understand the ache of leaving a child so far away. My friends cared, but they still had children at home.

Hudson seemed to be handling this empty nest thing better than I. He had retreated into his work as a way of not thinking too much. Cara and I talked each week—she was struggling with a demanding boss and a potential 'romantic interest' and suddenly, she needed to talk to me, to even ask advice! But she lived two hundred miles away. Fran called me, too, from college, when she could find a moment between sorority commitments, dates and—occasionally —her studies. I talked with my girls about their lives and then we hung up as they hurriedly said, "Love ya, Mom!"

I felt stuck in my old life but wanting to be a part of theirs. Wanting to be with them and knowing I could not, should not, intrude. Worry, wait and pray. Worry less, pray more.

One day, after I had returned from the library and was deciding what to fix for dinner, Sunny started barking excitedly and I thought to myself, Peter's home! Then I remembered that he was in college ten hours away.

I went about my routines. I transferred the laundry from washer to dryer—the first load I had done all week, and there were eight pairs of Hudson's underwear and seven of mine, a few of his T-shirts and some socks, but none of those wonderful teenage boy's clothes that had littered the house until a few weeks ago. I went to the store and bypassed the shelves with the cookies and the cereals and the stuff of boys. I spent $10 on sending Peter a package in the mail, I called his phone number without response, and everywhere, at the most unexpected times, I got that nauseous ache, that emptiness, that missing. Missing what?

The presence of my children, of Peter.

Even if my days were still pretty much the same, it was the nights that used to force me out of myself and into Peter's life. He needed a good dinner, he needed folded clothes, he needed encouragement on homework, he needed to talk or have his back scratched, and now, he was not here. And it was hard.

In the midst of this transition, I started having hot flashes. Sometimes I woke in the middle of the night drenched in sweat. My mind seemed to have turned to mush overnight. I suddenly could not remember the phone number of a publishing house I called once a month. I lost my keys, and found them in the refrigerator. Twice in one week at the library, I found myself standing in an aisle with a book in my hand and no idea what I was looking for.

Hudson teased me good-naturedly. I had nothing good-natured in me. I cried easily and I yelled at him—something I had rarely done in our 24 years of marriage. He learned quickly not to tease. In fact he tiptoed around me.

But Sunny was there. He was always happy to see me, to follow me around, to fetch the ball when I'd wander outside, my mind threatening to spiral into sadness or depression. I threw the old baseball and let tears run down my face as Sunny dashed across the yard to retrieve it. Inevitably his antics, so simple but intense, done with such pure pleasure, made me smile and laugh and want to live again.

Sunny was waiting for Peter, but he seemed perfectly content with me, too.

Chapter 27

The Good Woman seemed more emotional than usual. Her children, the Girls and My Boy, had gone away. She and the Big Man still left the house in the morning. She came home in the afternoon and he returned in the evening. During the day, the Good Woman smelled of loneliness. She was not an idle woman; she painted or she worked in her office where she sat in front of a big box and pecked with her fingers at little black squares. She also baked things that sent enticing odors throughout the house. She was busy, but she was sad.

One day she received a letter. I always warned her when the Letter Man drove up on his motorcycle and left things in the box by the driveway. The Letter Man was actually quite kind, but I still enjoyed barking at him.

On this day, she held the letter in her hand and began to cry. The liquid escaped from her eyes. She sat outside on the Bench, and I hopped on it beside her. She did not scold me. As I rested my head in her lap, I smelled something wonderful. My Boy! The paper she held in her hands smelled like My Boy.

I wanted to tell her not to be sad, that this was a good sign. Still she cried.

Chapter 28

The yard was mowed, and the last of the petunias poked their bright pink and purple heads out of the terra cotta pot on the wall. The yellow berries on the tree testified to fall as did the yellow leaves—only a few—here and there. Three pears from our tree lay on the green bench where Sunny was perched, asleep. Hudson and I started a project, painting the downstairs bedroom. He had suggested it as a way to get my mind off of Peter, and I agreed.

And so gradually, I wandered back to 'home' and found comfort in simple things. The dark thoughts and musings about my place in this empty nest lessened. My hot flashes did not. Friends came over and commiserated with me about menopause and missing children and I learned another truth about transition periods in my life. As an introvert, I needed 'down time' away from others to regroup and refresh and rejuvenate. But if I had too much time alone, then I dried up. I also needed time with other people to be reminded that the Lord had splashed the sin-stained canvas of this world with beautiful colors of relationship.

Empty-nesting seemed like a roller coaster ride, and though I learned how to function and adjust to the changes, my emotions were sometimes stuck far behind. I felt my Lord prying my fingers open again and again and again. I saw how terribly I wanted everything to be 'okay' for those I loved, how I wanted to protect and assure and control. Oh yes, control. For Peter.

His life was harder to control when he was thousands of miles away. I prayed, Help me, Lord, to be what he needs right now—a mother who prays and encourages and lets her son fly on his own, even if that means a few crashes along the way.

But it was hard! I wanted to help him organize his life. Cara and Fran had natural organizational skills. Peter was different. He had come so far, but I heard the lack of self confidence creeping into his voice during a phone conversation where he talked about trying out for the soccer team and the chorale. I wanted to help him and there was nothing I could do but listen and pray and write another letter on the bright, cheery stationery I bought at the store.

Sometimes I just wanted to fly in and have a party for Peter and any other lonely boys in their dorms who were feeling homesick. But he did not need 'Mama to the rescue'.

Eventually he made friends and his voice sounded confident and excited. He always asked about Hudson and me, but this was pure politeness. What he wanted to know, on every phone call, was, "How is Sunny?"

Chapter 29

My Boy did not come home for a long, long time. I spent my days between the house and the yard, following the Good Woman wherever she went. Soon after Peter left, something strange happened in the front yard. I had never been allowed to play there alone. The Good Woman knelt down and attached something to my collar. I thought she was going to take me on a walk, and I began to bark and wiggle. But she didn't attach a Leash. The Big Man led me to the edge of the front yard and said, "Stay!" Then he and the Good Woman walked into the street. Of course, I was eager to follow. I ran after them and was jolted by a force I couldn't see or smell, but could feel. If I walked too close to the street or to the yard next to us, I felt a horrible zap, zap, zap that stung and made me yelp in pain. The Good Woman came to me and tried to explain something. I never understood her, but I learned quickly to stay within the perimeter of our front yard, even when the humans left.

I actually enjoyed the new freedom and chance to explore another place. Outside, I chased squirrels that hopped to the ground from the trees, and I occasionally scurried after a chipmunk. I also talked with Bucky, an old golden retriever who lived next door. He too was forced to stay in his yard because of the invisible zapping machine. I lay in the sun and snapped at flies and waited for the Good Woman. I would lift my muzzle in the air, sniff and imagine My Boy there beside me. I found a baseball I had buried a very long time ago when My Boy had let me play in the front yard. I gnawed on it while I thought of him.

I was sleeping on the porch on a warm day after the daffodils and tulips had wilted and the yard was thick with the scent of honeysuckle. I heard a car come up the street and turn into the driveway. I lifted my head, tilted it just so as I concentrated on the sound of the car. Then I saw it. I knew that car! The Good Woman came out of the house, talking in a high-pitched happy way. I jumped to my feet and barked in the high pitched way I do when I am particularly excited. I made it to the car just as My Boy stepped out, and I planted my front paws on his chest. He laughed and said the name he always used for me. "Sunny!"

He was back! Once again our days were spent together, My Boy coming down the stairs in the morning and scratching my belly with his foot. We wrestled together on the freshly cut grass and he sat beside me on the Bench, his big hand on my back, stroking it and speaking to me in soft tones. My Boy had gained confidence far away from me. I rested my head in his lap and enjoyed his attention. I did not know where he had been, but I was happy he was back.

Chapter 30

That first summer when Peter returned from college was like a leisurely picnic of laughter and good food. The boy and his dog acted as if only seven months had passed since Sunny came to live with us, instead of seven years. Peter had buckled down and studied hard during his freshman year and was on track to get to vet school. He oozed a new confidence in himself and a new kindness—something we had always seen when he was with Sunny, but had not necessarily experienced for ourselves. He spoke with enthusiasm about becoming a vet, even though it was years away.

"No table food for Sunny, Mom!" he warned. "Make sure you take him out for a walk at least three times a week. He's in good shape, but you've got to make sure he doesn't gain weight."

After Peter left to return to college for his sophomore year, Hudson, Sunny and I settled back into our routine. I tried to obey Peter's instructions and took Sunny for walks and gave him only the best dog food. But I had to face it—he was definitely aging. The hair around his eyes and muzzle was a whitish-gray. He was going blind in one eye. He could no longer leap into the air to dislodge a sock that Hudson had tucked onto a branch of the pear tree. He used to jump into the hatchback trunk of the car with one energetic bound. Now it took several tries for him to get in. He almost looked embarrassed, as if to say, I'm so sorry. I know it's foolish, but I just can't make my body do this any more.

That's what I felt like saying, too. I knew dogs aged seven times as quickly as humans, but lately, I seemed to be catching up with him. I looked in the mirror one day and was surprised at how many gray hairs I found. Highlights could no longer cover them up, and so I made an appointment to get it colored. Sunny, of course, was not nearly as worried about his appearance as I was, although he certainly did like to lick himself clean. Lick, lick, lick and often at the most inopportune times, like when Hudson was asking the blessing and guests were at the table.

We had both gotten a little rounder, Sunny and I. Yes, we took walks, and we tried to be careful about what we ate. I cut down on his portions and gave him absolutely no table food as Dr. Tyler, the vet, and Peter ordered. Still weight gain seemed to be a part of the aging process. He looked at me with hungry, pleading eyes. When I fixed dinner, he was there beside me, hoping for a crumb to tumble to the kitchen floor where he could inhale it as my ever faithful vacuum cleaner.

How thankful I was to have Sunny there to keep me company. With all the kids gone and Hudson traveling more than ever, Sunny's loyal presence reassured me. Sunny stayed right beside me throughout the day, even when I broke into a sweat with my hot flashes and rushed outside for relief. He followed me, every step.

We were aging, but at least we were doing it together. I couldn't help but wonder how much longer Sunny would be with us. Dogs didn't live forever. I ached to even think of it. When I was a child, I literally got physically sick whenever one of our many animals died. I could not even imagine this life without Sunny.

I never thought that I would be lonely. I had so many activities. But empty nesting wasn't easy after all. Hudson and I had tried to keep communication open throughout the years. We'd talked, we'd loved. We even still liked each other, which was more than I could say for some of my couple friends. But he was gone a lot, and I was lonely.

I knew that Sunny missed Peter, but he actually seemed content just to be alone with me. I tried to get my mind around this. For the past eight years, I'd realized so much more about the Lord through our mutt. It sounded crazy, but it was true. And what I learned from him in the empty nesting time was this: Sunny waited for Peter, but he also enjoyed life while he was waiting. He really did.

There he was, lying in the grass, ears down, eyes closed, just relaxing. Then he heard a sound and he perked up and the ears went forward, and he was attentive. Then the mailman came by and he jumped to his feet, barking and racing to the fence. After 'protecting' me, he went back to his spot in the sun and napped again. He was content.

And he followed me everywhere, and that was okay too. He just wanted to be with me. I didn't get the feeling he was sad or depressed. He was just doing instinctively what he was supposed to be doing.

As I waited for my children, as I waited for the Lord to show me the next step in life, I wanted to go about my business, trusting Him to show up at the right time, and until He did, I wanted to be content in obeying what I already knew.

Chapter 31

My Boy often drove away in his car just when the blackberries were ripening and the fields behind the house had that yellowing color, the smell of wheat and summer ending. I had come to recognize the signs of a long departure. Bags were dragged from upstairs to the hallways and onto the porch. Then the car trunk was opened and in went the bags. Even though I wanted to jump into the trunk with Peter's belongings, as I had done on his first trip away from me, I could no longer make my body move in that way. So I just sat beside the car and looked at My Boy. I got up and paced, then I lay down again. I felt nervous when I knew the humans were leaving with bags—especially when I smelled his bags. I paced on the porch, I sat and stood, I lifted my muzzle to smell the weather. My Boy left when the sun still baked the grass in the day, when the leaves were still flickering on the trees and the butterflies still landed on the bushes until I chased them away. This was the season when he left.

He knelt down beside me and hugged my neck and I think his eyes were liquid. He spoke softly. He sat there stroking me and I wanted again to protect him, to journey with him and keep him safe and share adventures with My Boy.

But I could not go with my master on this journey. So I promised him with my eyes, that I would wait for him here, until he came back the next time.

Chapter 32

The Good Woman took me on walks almost every day. Sometimes, the Big Man joined us when the sun had fallen and the air was dark. But usually, I was alone with her. The Good Woman was not as strong as My Boy or the Big Man, so when we walked, I often pulled ahead, catching a scent of where Bucky or another dog had marked his territory. Of course I needed to cover over this with my own. I rushed ahead and sprayed the bushes or a tree or a bright mailbox so that the other dogs knew I had come by. I wagged my tail and yanked when I spotted a squirrel, frozen on the tree, head pointed down, little heart beating fast.

She liked to walk me down one street to where it opened into a park. Sometimes, the park was filled with other dogs and she would unleash me to play with them. Occasionally I felt threatened by a new male and tried to attack him, which scared the Good Woman. So once in a while she kept me on the Leash in the park.

On this day, I saw the dogs far on the other side of the park, I smelled their scent, I whined to tell the Good Woman that we needed to be careful. I pulled on the Leash, trying to get loose to meet the strangers. I barked and pulled harder. I could tell that the Good Woman was afraid when she saw the three dogs heading toward us, all of them unleashed. A German Shepherd, a Doberman and a terrier. Three males, coming for me!

The Good Woman yelled something to the man who was running behind, calling out frantically for the dogs to stop. But the German Shepherd, a young dog, approached me, tail wagging hesitantly. I bared my teeth and growled, then lunged forward to show him I was serious about protecting the Good Woman and myself. He did not pay attention, but walked right up to me.

This had always been something that scared me terribly, almost more than smelling a Bad Man—being held on a Leash when another male dog was loose and threatening.

My tail went straight up and the fur on my back stood up too. I snarled; he did not back away. I jerked away from the Good Woman and pounced on the German Shepherd, grabbing him by the throat. He yelped and shook free and then lunged at me. I could hear the Good Woman screaming at me, and I felt her tugging on the Leash, but I could not be bothered by things like collars and leashes when I was protecting myself and others. Before I knew it, the Doberman and terrier had jumped on me too. I realized that these three dogs could crush me with their combined strength. But fear spurred me on, and by the time the owner arrived, I was engaged in a terrible Fight with the three other males.

Those dogs knew how to fight.

I went for the Shepherd's throat again. I missed, but sank my teeth into his side and tasted his blood. He howled and shook and pulled back, growling and then lunging again at me. I was knocked on my side by the Shepherd and then the Doberman dove at me. I felt a terrible shock of pain and knew my opponents now tasted my blood. We rolled and thrashed, our legs tangled in the Leash. Then the other dogs went again for my throat and the teeth sank in and I fell back...

Chapter 33

He may have been getting older, but Sunny never really calmed down. Neurotic dog. Why should I have been surprised? When humans grew up around abuse, their lives were scarred. I believe Sunny was forever scarred by some events he endured as a puppy. For all of his life, he felt threatened by strange men and strange dogs.

Peter was in his last year of college when Sunny's worst fight took place. I was walking with Sunny in the park when I recognized the telltale signs of his fear. His red tail went up in a flash of thick fur, on display like a rooster's. He whined and then growled and then began to bark incessantly, all the while yanking on the leash. Coming toward us, tail high, but wagging, was a young German Shepherd, followed by a Doberman and a fox terrier. All males with no leashes, and the owner far away, running across the field and yelling, "Rocco! Bailey! Daisy!"

"My dog will attack him!" I yelled back, clutching at Sunny. "It's okay, boy. Heel! Stay!"

But the other dogs were now wary too. They braced themselves on stiff legs, whined and circled Sunny even as I tried to pull him away. Sunny lunged at the shepherd and a bona fide dog fight ensued. It seemed to last for hours, although probably only a few minutes passed before the other owner, a young man, managed to grab Sunny by the muzzle and drag him away from his own dogs. When we finally got them separated, the terrier and Doberman were fine. The Shepherd was bleeding, but not hurt badly, only a little bloody where Sunny took a mouthful of flesh.

But Sunny had a deep gash in his throat and another by his eye. I felt a horrible clutching in my stomach as I examined his injuries where he lay on the ground, whimpering. I murmured a prayer, "Dear Lord. Help him, help us. This is bad."

I pulled off my sweater and tried to stop the bleeding. A woman who had witnessed the fight offered to drive me to the vet's, since my car was sitting in our driveway half a mile away. Sunny could not walk back to the house, of that I was sure.

I held his head in my lap in the backseat as she drove to Dr. Tyler's. The gash above Sunny's right eye was deep and that eye remained closed, but he fixed his left eye on me. "Crazy old mutt. Couldn't you see you were outnumbered? Now look what you've done to yourself." I actually was fighting back tears, feeling sick to my stomach. Hudson and I had once talked about how we would handle it if we had to put Sunny down. More importantly, how would Peter handle it? Now it seemed a real possibility.

"Lanie," Dr. Tyler, the vet—who was by now a family friend—said to me, "your dog has lost a lot of blood. I can stitch up the gash over his eye, but the throat is going to require surgery."

The surgery cost $2000 with only a 50% chance of it being successful.

I had to make a decision. Spend $2000 on Sunny or let the vet put him down.

I called Hudson at his office and sobbed out the whole story. After a moment, he simply said, "I think we know what has to happen, dear, but you need to talk to Peter first."

After the third try, I got Peter on the phone. I explained the whole episode with a lump in throat. "It's not sure he would pull through, even with the surgery, Pete. Your dad and I think it would be more humane to put him down."

There was a long silence. "Tell Dr. Tyler to operate, and I'll pay for it. I have some savings, Mom." He had a desperate sound in his voice. "I'll be there tonight. You cannot put him down, Mom. He'll pull through."

Peter jumped in his car and drove ten hours straight to the vet's, arriving at two in the morning.

Sunny survived the three-hour operation. Dr. Tyler stayed with him at the clinic until Peter showed up. I'll never forget Dr. Tyler's words. "When Sunny saw Peter, even though he was shot through with anesthesia and bandaged so tightly he could barely move, he began to bark and wag his tail. Life returned to his eyes. I don't know if I've ever seen a dog who loved his master more."

Dr. Tyler left Peter at the clinic where our son stayed throughout the night, cradling Sunny's head in his lap. The next morning Dr. Tyler assured us that Sunny would make it, albeit with a nasty scar on his head and throat. That was quite all right with us.

Peter paid the bill with the money he had made during the summer—money he had hoped to save for vet school. I offered to help cover the cost. Peter looked at me with his dark, somber eyes and said, "I'm gonna be a vet, Mom. If I can't even save my own dog, what's the point? After all, he saved my life first—before I ever even thought it was worth saving. Nothing's too much to pay for Sunny."

"I know that, son." And I did.

Chapter 34

Peter came to care for me after the Fight. At the clinic, he held me and changed my bandages and fed me. When I went back to the house, I was too weak to stand up, so we sat together on the Bench. He held that old baseball and let me gnaw on it. At night, Peter brought his old sleeping bag, the one that still smelled like adventures in the woods, and slept on the floor by the steps where I rested. He put the backpack that the Bear had clawed in between us, and throughout the night, he'd reach into the bag and pull out something—a rag to dab where blood had seeped through the bandages, a tender dog nugget, a cool cloth that he wiped over my face.

When he left me, he had liquid in his eyes, and he spoke in a voice that cracked, which always meant he was sad. I tried to wag my tail and let him know it was okay. I had gotten used to him leaving. I didn't like it, but I had learned I could always trust him to return. Knowing that, I didn't mind waiting.

I was not completely healed when Peter left, so the Good Woman stayed home in the mornings with me, watching over me, almost as carefully as Peter. Gradually I began to walk. I could not see out of one eye, but the vision in my other eye was perfect. In the afternoons, I lay outside on the Bench and listened to the squirrels scurrying around and the blue jays gawking at each other and the bees hovering over the Good Woman's flowers.

Peter came back to me when the days were growing hot and long, and as always he left before the leaves started to fall from the trees.

When the air grew colder, I chased brittle leaves that flittered across the yard and then the Good Woman invited me inside to sit with her, beside the hearth where a hot fire burned. I used to bark at the bright flames, afraid they would escape from their Cage and hurt the Good Woman. But I learned that she liked the fire, liked sitting in front of it with a big book in her lap and her hand dangling over the side of the chair as she scratched my head.

My humans did strange things when the air got really cold and the days grew short. They brought a big spruce Tree into their home and wrapped little twinkling lights around it and hung shining balls all over it. I was never allowed to spray the low limbs with my urine. In fact, they sometimes yelled, "Sunny, stop!" when I walked by the Tree, wagging my tail. I obeyed, stopped, tail still wagging and swishing the limbs. Usually a crash followed where one of the little dangling balls fell to the ground. This unnerved me, but I still wagged my tail and tried to be friendly. The humans kept yelling and then laughing and finally Peter pulled me away from the Tree and into his lap, which was where I wanted to be in the first place.

The Tree always ended up with all sizes of colorful boxes pushed under it, boxes that I used to play with and chew until I found out that this made me a 'Very Bad Dog'. That lesson I learned soon after I came Home with My Boy, long ago. The Tree—or Trees, for a different one appeared each winter—meant that the Good Woman and the Big Man and the Girls and Peter all gathered together. In the later years, it meant that the Good Woman baked and decorated and sang happy songs because her children were coming back Home. More recently, the Girls had brought males back home with them. Cara brought Jim and Fran brought Samuel and after I had barked at them for a while, I grew to know them too.

And Peter. Peter always came home when the Tree had been in the house for a little while.

One cold day, when the Tree was up, Cara came to the house with a tiny human being in a funny little chair that she carried by the handle. The little human—they called her 'Baby'—worried me greatly. She squealed, which hurt my ears, and she screamed and cried—which hurt them even more. Cara was very protective of the Baby and never let me near the little human. I was so curious; I wanted to see this small human who made more noise than all of the regular humans put together.

All of my humans loved to hold the Baby. I didn't mind usually, because it meant the Baby didn't squeal and cry as much. But when Peter took the Baby in his arms, I did not like it. I whined and then I came to him, jumped up and wrapped my legs around his leg. Did My Boy need to be reminded that he belonged to me?

"Down, Sunny! Down." Peter scolded. But it worked. Peter gave the Baby back to Cara, and he let me sit by his side. I flopped over on my back and he rubbed my stomach.

The next time the Baby came to my house, it was bigger. It crawled on the floor and tried to take my food and put its hands in my water bowl. I did not much like this Baby. It pulled my tail and twisted the hairs in its fat little hands. Sometimes, it smelled of urine and excrement, which intrigued me. Usually humans did not have such pronounced smells. The Baby bothered me, but I knew that this was another human to whom I must be loyal.

Once, when Cara was gone and the Good Woman was holding the Baby, she knelt down and called me over. With my wet muzzle, I sniffed the tiny human. Then I licked its hand. It made a happy, giggling sound which did not hurt my ears. In fact, I enjoyed that sound. I decided that I liked the smell of the Baby after its bath, when it had the scent of powder on its skin and fresh honeysuckle in its hair. So I had one more human to love and protect.

Chapter 35

During Christmas break of Sunny's thirteenth year, Cara and Jim were here with little Trish—who was toddling around very well. Fran had brought her boyfriend, Samuel, whom we all liked a lot. Cara and Fran bustled around the kitchen with me, preparing Christmas goodies. And Peter came home for a whole month! His second year in vet school seemed to be going so well. He warned us that the hardest part was yet to come and his biggest exams were at the end of June. He wasn't sure when he would get home again for quite a while. I refused to think about that. We were all together now.

Sunny had grown to love Trish, going over to her and trying to lick her hands which made Cara extremely nervous. "He might hurt the baby," she said every time she had the chance. So Peter bought Sunny a fancy kind of harness—the kind that would not hurt his neck—which he used on Sunny to keep him from getting too close to Trish, and to take him on walks—very slow walks—to the park. I wouldn't have been surprised if good old Sunny still had it in him to attack another dog. His eyesight was bad and he could barely walk, but he still barked when the postman came by and he growled pretty convincingly at the beagle from way down the street who walked by the house in the evenings with his owner.

Still, we all admitted the truth. Sunny was old.

I knew that Peter would have a hard time leaving his dog this time.

On Christmas Eve, we were all eating our fancy meal in the dining room. Cara had put Trish to sleep on the bed in the guest room and surrounded her with pillows. She shut the door behind her to keep out the noise, sending Jim in to check on her periodically. At one point in the meal, I thought I heard Trish cry out from down the hall. She seemed to calm quickly, so we continued the meal. The next time Jim went to check, he came back with the sweetest expression on his face. "Y'all have to see this."

Sunny, old as he was, had still managed to open the door to the guest room and somehow climb onto the bed and lay down beside the baby, making a barrier with his body to keep Trish from tumbling off the bed. She was snuggled up sound asleep beside Sunny. When the rest of us came into the room, Sunny looked around with that furtive glance that asked if he was in trouble. He lowered his head and wagged his tail, very slowly, tentatively. No one scolded him. I thought Cara might get hyper and worry about germs, but she had a different reaction, watching the dog and the toddler. Her eyes glistened and she reached down and petted Sunny and whispered, "Dad was always right, you silly old dog. You're a real keeper."

Peter got his camera and took pictures which Sunny posed for in a regal manner. Trish continued sleeping peacefully. So Sunny worked his way into another heart.

Chapter 36

I have grown used to the Baby. I have grown used to all of them being at the house again. The Good Woman seems so happy with Cara and Fran and Peter and the others back at home. The house is filled with wonderful odors of meat and spices. Everyone sneaks me pieces of turkey. Music plays and candles burn and Peter stays near me. I move more slowly and I cannot see as well as I used to, but my sense of smell is still keen. I know My Boy by his touch and his smell. He takes care of me; Peter seems to know just what will make my muscles feel less sore and how far to take me on a walk. He sits beside me on the kitchen floor and I eat from his hand. He gives me a bath and then dries me with a big fluffy towel that I am pretty sure is only for humans. He even brings me upstairs to his room and I lie by his bed. The Big Man and the Good Woman do not seem upset. I sleep by his bed at night and I sit in his lap on the Bench in the day, both of us bundled under many blankets. I am content.

But My Boy is worried. I sense that he is worried for me. I wag my tail and nuzzle his hand and let him scratch my tummy. I don't want him to worry. What could be better than this? I am with My Boy.

When he tells me goodbye and loads his little car with the suitcases, he does not try to brush away the liquid in his eyes. He pets me and hugs me and says over and over and over again, "Sunny is a good dog. A good dog."

Chapter 37

For the past three days, Sunny hasn't eaten. I sit with him and hold his head in my lap and let him drink water out of my hand. Even this seems too much of an effort. Dr. Tyler said I would know when it was time.

Peter is in the midst of his exams, the big ones after his second year of vet school. He's called twice in the past week to check on Sunny. I tried to sound nonchalant. "He's pretty old, but hanging in there." Now I wonder if I have done the wrong thing. Peter must see his dog one last time.

I remember Peter's smoldering eyes, years ago, the first time I mentioned Sunny was aging.

I pick up the phone, and I dial Peter's number. I tell him I'm praying for him, for his exams. I ask how the studying is going. He says it's rough and that he can't wait until it's over. Only 48 hours left until he finishes all of his exams.

I ask him what he plans to do after the exams. He tells me he is going out with friends and that's when I suggest he might think of coming home for a few days. "Sunny seems to be slowing down pretty rapidly."

"Mom, what's wrong?" I hear the fear in his voice.

"Nothing dear, he's just old. Don't you worry, but perhaps you could come celebrate the end of exams with us." I am clearing my throat a lot, and Peter knows. He is not dumb. He is wrestling.

"Peter, you stay and take that exam, you hear me? I'll take good care of Sunny. I'll take him to see Dr. Tyler if he needs to. Don't worry. Put it out of your mind. Concentrate on the test."

Chapter 38

I can no longer muster the strength to stand up. I have tried ten times today, each time failing. She holds my head in her lap, strokes me gently, and gives me water in her hand. I cannot eat. My breathing comes in long, painful gasps. I see in her eyes that my suffering is hurting her too.

I think I am ready to close my eyes. It did not happen as I had hoped, and yet, these last days have let me relive all the other days with him, with My Boy. Humans don't always understand the depth of our loyalty, the necessity of belonging. I have belonged and I am content. I cannot even wag my tail to let her know that it is okay. I see the liquid spilling down her face and that always means she is hurting.

I have also wondered, because that liquid was on her face so often these last times, if something happened to My Boy. If in fact, he could not make it home. It has been so long. I cannot count time. I only remember that the last time he was with me, him sitting spread-eagled on the floor with me lying in between his legs and him petting me, I felt stronger. I could still bark. I couldn't run, but I did walk beside him twice.

Now it seems that nothing in my body works. I cannot even mark my territory.

Chapter 39

I carry Sunny out to the bench in the sun. It is a mild day. I believe it will be his last and so I want him to be outside where he perched so often, with the sounds and smells he loves. We sit on the bench, me singing the lullabies I used to sing to Peter so long ago. I don't know why I am singing lullabies to a dying dog.

There is nothing left to do but pray. It is the same prayer, over and over, "Let him get here in time." But I refuse to call him. He must finish his exams and then he will come. I cannot do anything else nor can I beg Sunny to hold on longer. He has struggled mightily and now it is time. I will ask Hudson to take him to the vet with me. I will stay right with him while Dr. Tyler lets him go.

Chapter 40

I am lying on the Bench in the sun. I can no longer see, my eyes having finally failed me, but I can still hear and I can smell. I smell life, the life of the place I love, the smell of the Good Woman who has cared for me, the smell of her flowers in bloom, the sweet fragrance of them, and I hear the buzzing of a dozen bees, busily gathering the nectar. I hear other things, a bird, the yapping of that bothersome beagle down the street. I have not been outside in a while. His yapping does not irritate me now. He is calling to me, wondering where I am. I do not have the strength to answer.

He asks me about The Boy and what can I say? That I have waited for these times, waited well and that I know he cares and that he will come sometime.

But now I know he will not find me.

The Good Woman leaves me on the Bench, whispering something softly to me. I hear the sound of her bare feet in the grass as she goes into the house. Always before, I followed her, but I cannot today. I am content to be on the Bench.

I doze and once again I dream of him. The dream is so real I can almost smell him, I can almost hear his lopsided gait, the way he used to drag that leg ever so slightly. I see him young and smiling, reaching out to pet me. Perhaps this is how it should end, with the smell becoming ever stronger, ever more familiar, that same sweaty smell of hard work and great kindness that has belonged to My Boy ever since we first met.

The step becomes louder too, the uneven rhythm, the quickness that is his, too.

I awake from the dream, hearing the Good Woman yelling something. Her voice is high and emotional. She will cry again. There is a hand on my head, a nose nestled in my fur and there is the liquid wetness seeping into that place above my muzzle and then I know. I am not dreaming. He has come to me, at last.

I offer all I can, a feeble whine. He is stroking me so softly, so gently and whispering soothing words and crying as humans do. He smells of medicine and fatigue.

Now the Woman is beside him and they are whispering and touching each other and then touching me.

My Boy is stronger than I remember. He lifts me easily and carries me into the house. He places me on the cool floor and lets me lick his hand over and over again. It is all I can do, but it is enough. He knows. I know. I waited and he came and I am content.

Chapter 41

He came to us in autumn and he left us the same way, licking Peter's hand. He was weak, almost pitiful as he took those heavy last breaths, yet with dignity in his tired eyes. My son sat with Sunny for thirty-six hours, did not change clothes or eat any food. He sat and stroked his dog, and Sunny kept living, peacefully living and licking, licking as was his habit. Peter and Sunny sat there and they were content, and then, with one last lick and one last breath, Sunny was gone.

We didn't say much for those hours. I considered it a holy moment between Master and pet. I had to find something to keep busy. I started writing in a journal, remembering as best I could every crazy antic of this mutt, and of all that he brought us, all he brought Peter.

We buried him under the green bench, and I planted tulip bulbs for the spring and pansies in the fall. Sometimes now, as I sit on that bench and read a novel, I can almost feel his head in my lap, almost smell him. I hear myself whispering his name and then there is the inevitable catch in my throat.

I think back to all that Sunny gave me, how I gained hope as I watched my preteen son playing with him, how I felt reassured with Sunny frolicking beside teenaged Peter, following him on yet another adventure. I think of how Sunny helped me step gracefully into mid-life and empty-nesting and the delight he and I shared when the kids came back home—even with the grandbaby. He reminded me that tears were okay in the midst of transition and of how important it was to have a loved-one nearby to wipe—or lick—them away.

Mostly, he taught me to look at My Master differently. I hope I have learned to love Him more, respect Him more, enjoy His presence more. If I have— and I hope this doesn't sound heretical, but God did make dogs—it comes from twelve years of living with a neurotic mutt.

Peter spent a month with us before he started up his last year of vet school. He grieved his dog. When he left, he took that torn backpack with him and a small canvas I painted of Sunny and him sitting on the bench.

He called us the other day. Hudson and I held the phone between us and listened as Peter told us that he had passed his exams and had found a job as a vet's apprentice. In every word he pronounced, we heard the confidence of a young man who understood animals, suffering and the power of love between humans and pets. Between a boy and his dog. Hudson and I smiled and nodded to each other, knowing that Peter was going to make a great vet. All because of Sunny.

When we hung up the phone, Hudson kissed me on the forehead and whispered, "I told you that dog was a real keeper."

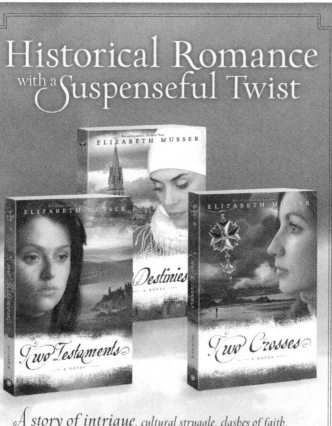

Made in the USA
Las Vegas, NV
15 September 2024

95332568R00056